MICHAEL MCGANN

THE MARKETISATION OF WELFARE-TO-WORK IN IRELAND

Governing Activation at the Street-Level

This research received funding from the European Union's Horizon 2020 research and innovation programme under the Marie Sklodowska-Curie grant agreement no. 841477. The views expressed are those of the author alone. The European Union is not responsible for any use that may be made of the information in this book.

POLICY PRESS SHORTS RESEARCH

First published in Great Britain in 2023 by

Policy Press, an imprint of
Bristol University Press
University of Bristol
1–9 Old Park Hill
Bristol
BS2 8BB
UK
t: +44 (0)117 374 6645
e: bup-info@bristol.ac.uk

Details of international sales and distribution partners are available at
policy.bristoluniversitypress.co.uk

British Library Cataloguing in Publication Data
A catalogue record for this book is available from the British Library

ISBN 978-1-4473-6705-5 hardcover
ISBN 978-1-4473-6706-2 ePub
ISBN 978-1-4473-6707-9 OA ePdf

Cover design: Bristol University Press
Front cover image: iStock/themacx
Bristol University Press and Policy Press use environmentally responsible
print partners.
Printed in CPI Group (UK) Ltd, Croydon, CR0 4YY

Contents

List of figures and tables

Figure

Tables

List of abbreviations

BOMi	Business Object Model implementation (information management system)
CE	Community Employment
DSP	Department of Social Protection
FÁS	An Foras Áiseanna Saothair (Training and Employment Authority)
GDP	gross domestic product
LES	Local Employment Services
NEAP	National Employment Action Plan
NPM	New Public Management
OECD	Organisation for Economic Co-operation and Development
PEX	Probability of Exit (from the Live Register)
PPP	Personal Progression Plan

About the author

Michael McGann is Lecturer in Political Science in the School of Social and Political Sciences, University of Melbourne. His main interests are in street-level bureaucracy and public service governance, with a particular focus on activation and employment services. His previous books include the co-authored *Buying and Selling the Poor: Inside Australia's Privatised Welfare-to-Work Market* (Sydney University Press, 2021). Although now based in Australia, Michael grew up in Dublin and continues to actively research social policy in Ireland.

Acknowledgements

This book is the culmination of a Marie Sklodowska-Curie fellowship, supported by the European Union's Horizon 2020 programme, and hosted by Maynooth University. I am indebted to the tremendous support I received from colleagues at Maynooth, particularly Mary P. Murphy who helped guide the project from inception through to conclusion. As anyone who has ever worked with Mary knows so well, Mary is an outstanding colleague and extremely generous collaborator. Her passion for transformative change is both inspiring and infectious, and it was a privilege to work with her on this and related projects. I am also grateful for the friendship and support of Nuala Whelan, who collaborated on parallel initiatives that did much to progress this project. Rhona Bradshaw, Orla Dunne, and Anne Hamilton also provided vital administrative support, along with Patrick Boyle and Edward Holden.

The book has also benefitted extensively from the periodic guidance of an advisory panel. It is not often that someone gets to deeply discuss their work with such an 'all-star' cast as Fiona Dukelow, Jo Ingold, Flemming Larsen, Colin Lindsay, and Muiris MacCarthaigh. I thank you all for the enormous time and rich advice that you each gave so freely.

More broadly, I would like to thank my long-standing Australian 'partners in crime': Mark Considine, Jenny M. Lewis, Siobhan O'Sullivan, and Phuc Nguyen. It was they who opened my eyes to the potential of street-level research, and the footprints of their formative impact on my career are littered throughout this book. More practically, the research owes much to their studies of the delivery of welfare-to-work in Australia, Britain, and beyond.

I would also like to thank the frontline staff and service-users who participated in the research and those within Turas Nua, Seetec, the Local Employment Services Network, and the Irish National Organisation of the Unemployed who helped facilitate the research. Without their support, this book would never have even gotten off the ground.

I am also grateful to everyone at Policy Press who helped bring this book to fruition, especially Laura Vickers-Rendall, Jay Allan, and Gail Welsh. Most of all, I am indebted to my family – Anna-Marie, Peter, and Rachel – for transporting their lives from Melbourne to Dublin to make this possible.

ONE

Introduction

This book addresses the transformations in welfare that have unfolded internationally since the 1990s, and more recently in Ireland. Specifically, the growing emphasis on reforming benefits and services to accelerate the targeting of claimants for 'activation'. Wacquant characterises this in terms of a 'shift from protective welfare, granted categorically as a matter of right, to corrective welfare' (2012: 72) conditioned on the fulfilment of conduct conditions.

What Wacquant terms 'corrective welfare', others term 'workfare' (Peck, 2001; Dingeldey, 2007; Brodkin, 2013b) – to emphasise the regulatory and 'work-first' orientation of contemporary activation (or welfare-to-work) policies. Benefits that once afforded a degree of protection from the vicissitudes of the market, and which partially de-commodified labour by enabling people to survive financially without employment, have increasingly been re-purposed as levers for recommodifying non-employed labour (Raffass, 2017). Labour market integration and the enforcement of citizens' dependency on (frequently low-paid) employment have eclipsed income protection as welfare's governing logic – symbolised in the redesignation of unemployment benefits as *jobseeker* allowances in several countries (Marston, 2006).

Alongside this repurposing of welfare have been important changes to role of states in service provision. Of key concern to this book is the withdrawal of governments from directly delivering public employment services in favour of contracting out the provision of employment guidance and job-search training services to non-government organisations. This has been an ongoing development across Organisation for Economic Co-operation and Development (OECD) countries for many years, taking varying shapes in different countries. Indeed, many countries have a long history of partnering with not-for-profit and community organisations to deliver programmes. What has changed more recently are the types of organisations being engaged to deliver public services. There has been a decided trend towards commissioning employment services via instruments of 'market governance' (Considine and Lewis, 2003: 133); procuring delivery through competitive tenders in which potential providers compete for contracts and receive payments predominantly based on the (employment) outcomes they deliver rather than the services they provide. This has seen for-profit firms rise to become major, and in some cases the dominant, providers of public employment services in several countries (Jantz and Klenk, 2015; Bennett, 2017; Considine et al, 2020b).

This book scrutinises the intersection between these two distinct but interrelated 'tracks' (Brodkin, 2013b: 11) of welfare reform; what, in shorthand terms, can be described as the 'activation turn' (Bonoli, 2010) in social policy and the governance turn towards marketisation in public administration. It sets out to consider not only why these two reform tracks have unfolded together but, more importantly, how they are mutually related in terms of marketisation propelling the policy turn towards a more conditional workfare model:

- Is it coincidence that as countries have looked to reconfigure their welfare systems to 'activate' claimants, they have frequently done so by transferring responsibility for service delivery towards private providers competing in quasi-markets?

• How does the delivery of employment services change in substance when enacted under conditions of market governance?

A street-level perspective

The book approaches these questions from the vantage point of street-level bureaucracy research, an approach to studying policy that was pioneered by Lipsky (2010) in the 1980s. For Lipsky, street-level bureaucracies constitute the government agencies that directly deliver programmes to citizens in a broad range of areas (social policy, healthcare, education, policing) and 'whose workers interact with and have wide discretion over the dispensation of benefits or the allocation of public sanctions' (2010: ix). It is this 'citizen-facing' role that separates them from other public organisations, although nowadays *non-government* organisations often perform this role. For this reason, contemporary scholarship tends to talk of street-level *organisations* rather than bureaucracies since policies 'may be delivered through a variety of organisational forms' (Brodkin, 2015: 5).

Street-level research begins from the perspective that politics and administration are inseparable. The 'being' of policies depends on how they are enacted by street-level organisations and the frontline staff working within them. This is an unsettling idea for public administration, which has a long history of trying to separate the partisan world of policymaking from the 'professional' field of policy implementation (Moynihan and Soss, 2014). But there are at least two reasons why studying policy at the street-level delivery is critical. First, most people encounter policy in embodied form through their experiences with specific caseworkers, clerical officers, and other agents of the state. So, to understand the impact of welfare reforms on citizens' lives we need to examine them not as they are 'in abstract regulations' (Rice, 2013: 1055) but as they materialise on the street. A second reason is the issue of administrative discretion. Street-level workers do not just implement policies as written. They shape, transform, and even make policy *while* delivering services. This stems from the degree of ambiguity marking policies in many cases, the space in between the rules.

Policies are rarely fully determinate about what should be done in each case. So, frontline workers must use their judgement to determine how general rules can be fitted to the nuances of real lives. Hence why street-level workers are often considered 'de facto policymakers' (van Berkel, 2013: 88; Brodkin, 2013a: 23) who continue the process of policymaking 'while policies are delivered' (Caswell et al, 2017: 2). This exercise of discretion is rarely uniform, but neither is it ad hoc. It is structured by the organisational routines, management, and performance regimes surrounding frontline work, as well as the kinds of professional identities, personal experiences, and worldviews that workers bring to their jobs. The challenge for students of street-level bureaucracy is to understand how these factors shape discretion 'and what that means for the production of policy' (Brodkin, 2015: 5), and ultimately for the citizen or service-user. This requires making sense of what Brodkin terms 'the missing middle' of policy analysis: 'the opaque spaces between formal policy provisions and social outcomes in which the essential work of the welfare state and its policies takes place' (2013c: 271–272).

Recognising this brings into view why governance reforms matter to determining the substance of activation. In reconfiguring *how and by whom* policies are delivered, governance reforms carry the potential to indirectly change *what* policies are produced. If politics is about 'who gets what, when, and how' (Lasswell, 1936), and governance reforms reshape these dynamics at the street-level, then the administrative is political!

Why Ireland?

To date, policy delivery in Ireland has rarely been a subject of street-level research. This book hopes to break new ground in this regard, but it is also motivated by the fact that the history of post-crisis welfare reform in Ireland offers an especially pertinent case study for examining the intersections between the 'activation turn' in social policy and the 'marketisation turn' in welfare administration. As detailed in Chapter Two, the country was historically an outlier among the group of liberal welfare states both for the relative passivity of its welfare state, as well as its weak commitment to New Public Management (NPM) style reforms. It was frequently chastised as a 'laggard' (Köppe and MacCarthaigh, 2019: 138) that was dragging its heels on activation reform. The Director of the OECD's Labour and Social Affairs division famously likened Ireland's pre-crisis activation model to 'the emperor who had no clothes' (Martin, 2015: 9) insofar as there was almost no use of sanctions and little implementation of conditionality.

All this has now changed, with social policy in Ireland widely argued to have taken 'an increasingly workfarist turn' (Gaffney and Millar, 2020: 69) since 2010; albeit one that has yet to reach the punitive heights seen in Britain or Australia. Yet, an unusual feature of how Ireland reformed its welfare state during this period was the government's 'pluri-governance' (McGann, 2022b: 942) approach to commissioning employment services for the long-term unemployed. Market governance was introduced on top of pre-existing corporatist structures and a long tradition of mixed welfare delivery through church and community organisations.

From 2015 until 2022, Ireland evolved an almost unique 'mixed economy' of activation that afforded a rare opportunity to directly compare otherwise equivalent employment services that were steered through contrasting governance modes. The details of this mixed economy are discussed in Chapter Two, but it essentially involved an entirely new service for the long-term unemployed (JobPath) developing alongside an existing network of Local Employment Services (LES) that had been operating since the mid-1990s. Most significantly, JobPath was procured through competitive tendering and delivered by two private firms on a Payment-by-Results basis. By contrast, LES were delivered by 22 not-for-profit organisations on a 'costs-met' basis without any competitive procurement. There was almost no use of market instruments to steer how LES were delivered, despite JobPath and LES both being contracted by the same administrative unit to deliver equivalent durations of support to much the same clients (people receiving jobseeker payments for at least 12 months or who were deemed at risk of long-term unemployment).

Ireland's mixed economy of activation was essentially a natural policy experiment in the use of different governance modes to steer frontline delivery. This book draws on original comparative research into this mixed economy – survey research and in-depth interviews with frontline JobPath and LES staff, qualitative research with service-users, and interviews with key officials – to assess the extent to which the use of market governance instruments changes the substance of policy delivery. Specifically, whether (and how) the procurement of employment services via market governance instruments spills into the delivery of a more demanding, workfarist model of activation at the street-level. It also examines the internal changes wrought by marketisation in how the performance of street-level workers is managed, monitored, and measured – and the effects on workers' professional identities – and how these reshape agency in policy delivery. The study is described in Chapter Three while the reforms that have unfolded since 2010 are reviewed in Chapter Two. First, it is necessary to elaborate on the broader international context and contours of what is dubbed the 'unfolding workfare project' (Brodkin, 2013b: 3).

The 'activation turn' in social policy

The past 30 years, Considine and Lewis argue, have seen a major 'sea change' (2010: 385) in how welfare is enacted. A key part of this has been the coupling of income supports with 'supply-side employability interventions' (Whitworth and Carter, 2020: 845) aimed at moving claimants into work. This so-called 'activation turn' (Bonoli, 2010: 435) has been heavily championed by the OECD, although there are important variants in how it has been implemented. One common typology is to differentiate the 'enabling' or 'human capital development' elements of activation (education and retraining) from the 'regulatory/demanding' or 'workfarist' elements including the use of benefit reductions, time limits on payments, and other negative incentives to push people into work (Dingeldey, 2007; Lindsay et al, 2007; Raffass, 2017; Whelan et al, 2021).

Human capital versus workfare models of activation

In practice, almost all labour market policies combine 'a mix of demanding and enabling elements' (Sadeghi and Fekjær, 2018: 78). Countries that prioritise building employability through upskilling will often make benefits conditional on participation in training. Nonetheless, in general terms, two distinct styles of activation can be coherently distinguished: a *human capital* model and a *workfare* model. While both aim at citizens achieving economic self-sufficiency through employment, they differ in their problem diagnosis and recommended course of treatment. They are also not the only activation models. Other alternatives include 'career-first' (Fuertes et al, 2021), 'work-life balance' (Whelan et al, 2021), and even 'life-first' (Dean, 2003) models. However, these remain little more than conceptual alternatives which have seldom been implemented.

The human capital model is associated with social-democratic welfare regimes, and the social investment 'paradigm' (Hemerijck, 2015: 242) that influenced the European Union's (EU) employment strategy in the early 2000s (de La Porte and Jacobsson, 2012). This approach pursues activation though education, training, and work experience initiatives that aim to develop the vocational skills and resilience of claimants to cope with structural economic changes and more flexible labour markets. Human capital models thus focus on the value of well-funded training and other 'skill-enhancing' (Sadeghi and Fekjær, 2018: 78) programmes as mechanisms for both reintegrating marginalised citizens into employment as well as enhancing the labour mobility of existing workers. From this perspective, activation programmes are seen as enabling labour market reintegration while also mitigating the risks of people falling out of employment into long-term joblessness. Moreover, the causes of unemployment are viewed in structural terms as being a mismatch between the skills demanded by employers and the capacities and resources of un(der) employed workers.

Workfare models, by contrast, try to catalyse transitions from welfare-to-work using policy instruments with 'more perceptibly hard edges' (Brodkin, 2013b: 6). Examples include the imposition of mandatory work obligations in the form of 'Work-for-the-Dole' programmes. Indeed, workfare is sometimes equated precisely with mandatory work programmes (Lødemel and Moreira, 2014: 9). However, most understandings adopt a wider definition of workfare as an activation model that focuses on combining tighter eligibility conditions for receiving payments with more onerous behavioural conditions backed by sanctions for claimants who breach obligations to seek and accept work (Bonoli, 2010). Workfare models will include some enabling measures (job-search training) to assist people in their search for work. However, the emphasis of even these enabling measures is on prioritising 'perpetual job-search motion' (Wright et al,

2020: 286) and rapid labour market attachment as the pathways to employment. Activation assumes the 'work-first' form of counselling people in how to job-search through a blend of 'services and sanctions' (Kluve, 2010), guided by the assumption that 'the best way to succeed in the labour market is to join it' (Lindsay et al, 2007: 541). The goal is to scaffold claimants into finding job vacancies that they can get with whatever skills and experience they already have – by increasing the efficacy and intensity of their job-searching – rather than developing the skills, qualifications, and/or work experience they need to obtain employment that matches their career goals.

In historical terms, the workfare model is associated with liberal welfare regimes. It originated in the United States (US) in the 1980s, spreading to Australia and the United Kingdom (UK) in the mid-1990s (Lødemel and Gubrium, 2014; O'Sullivan et al, 2021). But it would be a mistake to associate it exclusively with liberal welfare regimes. Indeed, since the early 2000s, there has been a discernible shift towards workfarist models across OECD countries as 'conditions and sanctions for the unemployed have overall become stricter' (Knotz, 2018: 92). It is a shift that has accelerated since the financial crisis, as more countries have reoriented their policies toward 'promoting the demanding elements of activation' (Seikel and Spannagel, 2018: 247). This has especially been the case in Britain, where the escalation in the use of welfare conditionality since 2010 – in terms of the severity of penalties and the onerousness of conduct conditions – has been likened to a brutalising regime of 'violent proletarianisation' (Grover, 2019). But it has also been the case in European countries previously committed to the human capital approach such as the Netherlands, Sweden, and Denmark (de La Porte and Jacobsson, 2012; Umney et al, 2018; Bekker and Mailand, 2019). To this extent, the workfare model is increasingly regarded as the 'standard welfare orthodoxy at the heart of international welfare systems' (Whitworth and Carter, 2020: 845).

The governance turn towards marketisation

Besides changes in payment rates, sanctions, and eligibility conditions, the institutional structures through which activation policies are implemented have also changed in important ways. As countries have reoriented their activation policies towards a workfarist blend of job-search services and sanctions, it has become rarer for programmes to be delivered by public organisations or to be coordinated through traditional forms of bureaucratic accountability. Employment services are instead increasingly coordinated through new menus 'of incentives and regulatory devices' (Considine et al, 2015: 22) and enacted by a wider range of actors from across the public, private, and community sectors.

There are several strands to these governance shifts, which can be loosely grouped under the umbrella of 'NPM in activation' (Ehrler, 2012: 328). One helpful way of approaching NPM is as a blend between two related governance modes: 'corporate' and 'market' governance (Considine and Lewis, 2003). The former emphasises 'management by objectives' and steering organisational and individual behaviour through performance measurement and targets. Its core instruments are the setting of organisational goals and employee targets, developing systems for measuring performance, and incentivising goal-achievement through performance bonuses. Market governance is related to corporate governance in that organisations in public service markets will often use 'managerialisation' (Larsen and Wright, 2014: 457) to internally manage their staff. Nevertheless, what differentiates market governance is its prioritisation of 'management by competition'. Where corporate governance tries to transform the public sector by making it more like private enterprise, market governance seeks to abolish monopolistic state provision through creating markets for public services in which various for-profit, not-for-profit, and even public organisations compete. This is initially to win government contracts but then to attract clients from which they can derive service fees and outcome payments.

While corporate governance reforms are an important part of the reform story, it is the rise of quasi-marketisation that arguably constitutes the most significant of the governance reforms facing welfare states today (Greer et al, 2017; Jantz et al, 2018). It entails boundary setting reform that not only shifts the role of government from a provider of services to a purchaser of outcomes. It also profoundly reshapes the social divisions of welfare between the market, state, and community sectors.

What is driving this project of marketisation? That is a key question returned to throughout this book. Governments may have both pragmatic as well as ideological reasons for introducing quasi-markets. For instance, the state's internal capacity to deliver employment services may quickly become overwhelmed by a surge in unemployment owing to economic recession. Under such circumstances, outsourcing may afford governments a way of bolstering capacity while avoiding long-term cost commitments (Langenbucher and Vodopivec, 2022). This was an important consideration behind the Irish Government's commissioning of JobPath. But it does not fully explain why contracting out increasingly involves allocating services through forms of competitive tendering and outcomes-based contracting. That is, in addition to bringing on board external employment services capacity, why governments increasingly choose to do so through processes of competitive bidding and results-based payment models. This predilection for using market governance instruments in service commissioning stems rather from a normative belief in the utility of markets to promote 'a higher quality of service and a more efficient allocation of resources' (Le Grand, 2011: 84).

Quasi-markets in employment services

At this point, it is pertinent to elaborate on why public services markets are considered *quasi*-markets, and the diversity of forms they take. The expression 'quasi-market' captures how public services markets differ from private markets in at least three ways (Le Grand and Bartlett, 1993) relating to the motivations of the 'sellers', the degree of consumer choice over purchasing, and the concentration of purchasing power in the state.

Not all providers in quasi-markets are privately owned or driven by profit-maximisation. Many are purportedly not-for-profit organisations with a social mission, although what differentiates not-for-profit from for-profit providers is not always clear in practice (Considine et al, 2020b; O'Sullivan et al, 2021). There are also examples of quasi-markets with publicly owned providers, such as Australia's Job Network which was introduced in 1998 when the Howard government put the Commonwealth Employment Service into competition with private contractors. This started a slippery slope towards full privatisation in 2003, when the public provider lost all its contracts. So, while 'marketisation is not synonymous with privatisation' (Van Berkel et al, 2012: 275) it can certainly clear the way for a corporate capture of public services (Bennett, 2017). Much will depend on the extent to which state-owned services are exposed to competition and what steering instruments are used.

Key concerns are the degree of price-bidding permitted during tendering and the extent to which funding models are tilted towards Payment-by-Results rather than fees-for-service. Where bidders are encouraged to compete on price – bidding down the value of the fees and outcomes payments they stand to earn – this can skew quasi-markets in favour of larger firms who can use their economies of scale to outbid competitors. Likewise, if the funding model is oriented towards Payment-by-Results, this can similarly favour 'bigger, multi-national for-profit actors' (Langenbucher and Vodopivec, 2022: 11), as has been the recent experience in Australia and the UK (Considine et al, 2020b). Outcomes (or results)-based payment models essentially transfer the financial risk of service delivery onto providers. Large, for-profit firms can borrow capital in international markets to finance the upfront costs of Payment-by-Results contracts in the hope of generating a profitable return on their investment. This is a more difficult option for not-for-profit agencies; especially grassroots organisations whose boards may by unwilling or unable to assume the financial risk needed to manage Payment-by-Results contracts (Shutes and Taylor, 2014).

The second key difference between quasi-markets and conventional markets is that the ultimate consumers (claimants) rarely purchase services directly. In conventional markets, consumers reign sovereign to the extent that they enjoy the right to take their business elsewhere should they be dissatisfied with the service on offer. This consumer choice is a key dynamic that drives the purported efficiency of the market as an optimal means of allocating resources. Early theorisations of quasi-markets also celebrated the possibilities of unlocking consumer choice to increase service responsiveness on the grounds that: 'If users who are receiving a poor-quality service from particular providers can go elsewhere ... [and] the money follows the choice, then the providers concerned have a strong incentive to deliver a higher quality of service; for, if they do not, they will go out of business' (Le Grand, 2011: 85).

However, this kind of consumer purchasing power is seldom realised in welfare-to-work markets. Claimants rarely have the choice to 'go elsewhere'. More often, they are treated as passive clients that the state simply directs 'to the provision it has bought' (Wiggan, 2015a: 117). There are exceptions. Two notable examples are Germany and the Netherlands, both of which have experimented with voucher schemes whereby jobseekers are given tokens to purchase labour market reintegration services from their preferred provider. It is still the state that ultimately makes the purchase, but the use of vouchers does give jobseekers some say over which services are bought. However, experience to date suggests that consumer choice is often only weakly enacted even under such conditions. One reason is that claimants often have limited information by which to make an informed choice between providers. Another is that those with the most complex employment challenges tend also to be the least likely to exercise choice (Jantz and Klenk, 2015). It is for these reasons that van Berkel and colleagues conclude that it is generally 'not the case' (2012: 282) that quasi-marketisation empowers service-users' choice.

The final key difference between quasi-markets and conventional markets is the potential for purchasing power to be concentrated in a 'monopsony' (Struyven and Steurs, 2005: 215) purchaser. This is where a single government agency acts as the sole purchaser within the market, as has been the case in Australia for 25 years and likewise in Ireland, where all externally delivered services are centrally contracted by a single unit of the Department of Social Protection (DSP). This consolidation of purchasing power is problematic for maintaining a *competitive* market structure which, Struyven and Steurs argue, depends not only a diversity of providers 'but also a sufficient number of purchasers' (2005: 215).

In a fully competitive market, the quantity of services produced, and at what price, should be a function of the overall balance between supply and demand. In quasi-markets, however, the total level of demand for activation services is fixed by the government. While this doesn't give it complete control over price – it must offer prices that providers are willing to bid for – it does give it far greater leverage to dictate contract terms than in a competitive market. Again, there are exceptions to this rule of monopsony purchasing such as the Netherlands and Denmark, where responsibility for administering social assistance and coordinating activation services lies with municipal governments. Providers therefore have a wider range of purchasers that they can transact with, giving them potentially greater leverage to demand higher prices. Conversely, in quasi-markets with a monopsony purchaser, established providers that have already made sunken investments to deliver previous contracts can become 'locked-in' to tendering for future contracts through resource dependency (Taylor et al, 2016; Considine et al, 2020a).

Varieties of quasi-markets

Beyond consumer choice being more restricted in quasi-markets compared with conventional markets, it is also important to recognise that quasi-markets are 'not one thing' (Meagher and Goodwin, 2015: 3). They vary significantly between (and within) countries in terms of whether purchasing power is centrally consolidated in a single purchaser, the degree to which they embed privatisation, and the extent to which they enable user choice. This has led to a growing awareness that quasi-markets differ as much as they converge, and that their relationship to 'market governance' is variable (Gingrich, 2011; Van Berkel et al, 2012; Wiggan, 2015a).

One way of unpacking this variation is to distinguish between waves of quasi-marketisation. This helps to capture where and when quasi-markets first emerged, and how quickly they travelled elsewhere. Taking this approach, we can distinguish *pioneering countries* leading the turn towards quasi-marketisation from *early adopters* and *late comers*. Pioneering countries include:

- the US, where quasi-markets took root during the late 1980s (Finn, 2010);
- Australia, which began to outsource activation services for the long-term unemployed in 1994 (Considine et al, 2015); and
- the UK, which turned to quasi-markets to implement the Blair government's New Deal programmes in the late 1990s (Larsen and Wright, 2014; Jantz and Klenk, 2015).

The Netherlands is also sometimes considered as a pioneering reformer (see Finn, 2010), although a fully competitive market wasn't introduced in the Netherlands until the early 2000s (van Berkel and van der Aa, 2005). This was when several other European countries also turned to competitive procurement and outcomes-based contracting to reorganise their employment services. For example, in 2002, Denmark's newly elected centre-right government mandated that at least 10 per cent of all activation services for those on social insurance payments should be outsourced. Although it was left to regional agencies to determine which services should be contracted out and by what means (Larsen and Wright, 2014). Another 'early adopter' was Germany, which introduced a system of competitive tendering for the delivery of both job placement and training services in 2002–2003. In the German case, placement and training services were competitively procured through vouchers given to unemployed people by the Federal Employment Agency which enabled them to purchase services from their preferred provider as opposed to the state directly contracting providers.

A third group of countries might be classified as 'late comers' in that they embraced quasi-markets in employment services only well after they had taken root elsewhere. Ireland is an exemplar 'late comer' having turned to competitive tendering and outcomes-based contracting in 2015.

Table 1.1 summarises the spread of quasi-markets over time by pioneering countries, early adopters, and late comers. This is by no means an exhaustive list, and there are many countries not included (France, Sweden, Switzerland) which have also pursued market governance reforms of their employment services. It is intended merely as an indicative demonstration

Table 1.1: Waves of quasi-marketisation

Chronological stages	Examples
Pioneers	US (1980s), Australia (1994), UK (1997)
Early adopters	Netherlands (2001), Denmark (2002), Germany (2003)
Late comers	Ireland (2015), Finland (2015–2019)

of the extent to which different countries were at the forefront of, or lagged behind, the governance turn towards marketisation. Nonetheless, this chronological approach reveals a degree of correlation between the workfarist trajectory of countries' activation policies and their adoption of quasi-market implementation structures. The 'pioneering countries' are all Anglophone, liberal regimes renowned for their commitment to workfarist activation. The group of 'early adopters' includes countries that are more typically characterised as either social-democratic (Denmark) or corporatist-conversative (Germany) regimes. However, the period when these countries turned to quasi-marketisation is also when their active labour market policy settings shifted in a workfarist direction. In Germany, increasing marketisation from 2002–2003 onwards coincided with the Hartz reforms which sought to reduce benefits for the long-term unemployed, enable transitions into shorter-term and more flexible employment contracts, and reorient training programmes away from vocational training and further education towards shorter-term labour market training (Dingeldey, 2007). Likewise, in Denmark, the mandating of contracting out unfolded under a new centre-right government that also sought to shift the emphasis of Denmark's activation model 'from human capital development toward a workfare or work-first model' (Larsen, 2013: 103). From 2002, moving unemployed people into work at speed became the guiding logic of Danish activation policy, with an increased emphasis on using sanctions and jobseeker agreements to do so. The same is true of the 'late comers', as discussed in Chapter Two, raising the question of whether the intersection between the two reform tracks is merely coincidental, or whether marketisation and workfare are in fact 'two sides of the same coin' (van Berkel and van der Aa, 2005: 330).

Beyond differences in time, other typologies focus on how quasi-markets differ in terms of the extent to which they embed market competition (producer-driven) and user choice (consumer-driven) as key steering mechanisms or remain strongly regulated by the state (state-managed) as a vertical control on the autonomy of market providers (see Gingrich, 2011). Van Berkel et al (2012) differentiate 'committed marketisers' such as Australia and the UK from 'slow modernisers' such as Italy and the Czech Republic. In the former countries, market governance instruments play a central coordinating role. The level of outsourcing to private providers is very high, and the modes of contracting (competitive tendering, performance-based payments) favour allocating resources based on market governance instruments of price competition and Payment-by-Results. Providers are also only weakly regulated, and retain considerable leeway to determine the frequency, content, and even targeting of services in what is sometimes referred to as a 'black box contracting' approach: where the government purchaser concerns itself mainly with outcomes and 'allows the service provider to determine the workings, including staffing, style of interaction with clients, and the frequency and nature of the services provided' (O'Sullivan et al, 2021: 46).

'Committed marketisers' revolve around what Gingrich (2011) would classify as 'producer-driven' quasi-markets. Namely, quasi-markets in which decisions about the targeting and content of services lie mainly with providers rather than being shaped by the consumption patterns of service-users or the regulatory decisions of the state. They are quasi-markets in which service-users have few exit options and public managers take a 'hands-off' approach to regulation, believing that that 'producers will have more room to innovate where there is less state interference' (Gingrich, 2011: 17). Conversely, in 'slow marketisers' the overall level of outsourcing is low and many if not most services continue to be publicly administered through large state-owned agencies subject to hierarchical control. While quasi-markets may be a feature of these countries' activation systems, opportunities for new players to enter the market are rare and are tightly controlled by accreditation requirements (Jantz and Klenk, 2015).

In between 'committed marketisers' and 'slow modernisers' is a group of 'modernisers': countries such as Sweden and France where the governance of activation is more hybrid in form. There is a blend of service provision by different sectors, but contracted providers are also subject to a mix of accountability instruments, including not just financial accountability for results but also regulatory accountability for adhering to minimum servicing standards, equal access provisions, and other quality controls monitored by public administrators (procedural governance). In these instances, the introduction of quasi-markets does not lead to a major displacement of alternative governance modes. Rather, marketisation co-exists and intersects with procedural governance and even forms of network accountability as policymakers try to balance 'competition and freedom in delivery with control' (Jantz et al, 2018: 339) to avert some of the risks and unintended consequences of market governance models. Principal among these risks is the danger that providers will respond to outcomes-based payment models by engaging in practices of so-called 'creaming' and 'parking'. This is where, to maximise revenues and meet performance targets, providers concentrate their resources on their most 'job ready' clients. The jobseekers that they perceive as being closest to employment are met with more frequently, given more intensive employment guidance, and referred to more job vacancies. Conversely, those who are identified as having more complex needs are given little meaningful support beyond what's needed to earn registration payments.

Problems of 'creaming' and 'parking' are far from exclusive to quasi-markets. Facing limited resources, high caseloads, and pressures to meet targets, frontline staff in public agencies are also liable to engage in similar frontline 'selection practices' (van Berkel and Knies, 2016: 64). Nonetheless, several aspects of quasi-market provision including the for-profit motive of many providers and the contingency of providers' payments on achieving employment outcomes make guarding against practices of creaming and parking a 'perennial' (Carter and Whitworth, 2015: 113) challenge for quasi-markets. This is reflected in the extent to which practices of 'creaming' and 'parking' have been documented in a variety of quasi-markets internationally, including Australia (Considine, 2001), the UK (Greer et al, 2018), and the Netherlands (van Berkel and Knies, 2016). From the contractor's perspective, it is entirely rational to selectively concentrate their resources on those clients they believe can be more quickly placed into employment. However, it essentially results in a misallocation of public resources away from those who need assistance the most. Moreover, these frontline selection practices are far from random hitting certain groups such as older jobseekers and those with disability 'harder than others' (van Berkel and Knies, 2016: 63) and highlighting a key tension between equity and efficiency in quasi-market models. Paying for performance may come at the expense of purchasing services that are equally available to all who need them (Greer et al, 2017).

The nature of quasi-markets in modernising and slow marketising countries is more reflective of a 'state-managed' than 'producer-driven' market. Public managers use market instruments 'to set incentives for cost-efficiency' but the state intrudes in the market to set clear parameters on ' "meat and potatoes" issues' (Gingrich, 2011: 13) like staffing and caseload sizes. These will be tightly specified in contracts and enforced through close auditing of providers and issuing of financial penalties for breaches of minimum standards. State-driven quasi-markets thus blend market governance with strong forms of procedural accountability anchored in 'a legalistic structure with clear standards and tight control' (Gingrich, 2011: 14). They are less concerned with catalysing innovation than with harnessing the market to achieve cost savings. This is in sharp contrast to the degree of power ceded to market actors in 'producer-driven' markets, which involve the purest form of market governance and most radical change to the role of the state in welfare administration.

As discussed in Chapter Two, Ireland's JobPath lies somewhere between a 'producer-driven' and 'state-managed' quasi-market (Wiggan, 2015b). This is to the extent that the two providers were required to adhere to minimum servicing standards regarding caseload sizes and the frequency of appointments. Nevertheless, the procurement model actively encouraged providers to price-bid during tendering and the funding model was heavily tilted towards Payment-by-Results. Consequently, market forms of accountability had a decisive role in the allocation of services under JobPath, making it somewhat closer to a 'producer-driven' than 'state-driven' quasi-market.

Towards 'double activation'

Clearly, the recent history of welfare reform is not just about the push to convert claimants into active jobseekers through behavioural conditions and sanctions. Core to the contemporary workfare project is a parallel agenda of transforming how services are produced by street-level organisations; partly through opening public services to competition but also through using financial incentives to motivate providers to deliver services more efficiently and in different ways. This second reform track has become 'closely intertwined' (Brodkin, 2013b: 11) with workfare reforms, although it has varied between countries in pace and form.

As in the case of workfare policies, Anglophone liberal countries pioneered quasi-marketisation. Several European countries shortly followed as they too sought to dilute their earlier emphasis on human capital development in favour of a more workfarist model. Different countries organised their quasi-markets in different ways, varying the balance of power between the state, the market, and service-users. Nonetheless, in all cases, the project of welfare reform can be understood as being targeted 'at least as much at welfare-to-work providers and their caseworkers as at unemployed claimants' (Whitworth and Carter, 2014: 106). Put differently, it constitutes a project of *double activation* (Considine et al, 2015; McGann, 2021) where not just claimants but also the organisations and case managers responsible for implementing activation on the ground are being governed through 'incentives for right behaviour and penalties for non-compliance' (Soss et al, 2011a: 229). This concept of double activation lies at the heart of this book. It is discussed extensively in Chapter Three, which presents the case for treating 'double activation' as much more than a simple description of the parallels between how claimants, contracted providers, and the street-level workers are governed by the state. The real value of a double activation lens lies in its ability to interrogate how the first order project of claimant activation is influenced *and reshaped* by the administrative governance reform project of 'activating the organisations and frontline staff involved in policy implementation' (van Berkel, 2013: 100). Without the latter, the former workfare project would look very different.

The book proceeds as follows. Chapter Two builds on the analysis of the twin tacks of welfare reform to unpack how the post-crisis reform of the Irish welfare state proceeded through a blend of workfarist social policy reforms coupled with market governance (among other) administrative reforms of employment services institutions. Chapter Three then introduces the *Governing Activation in Ireland (GAII)* study underlying this book in the context of elaborating the concept of 'double activation' and developing an account of the conceptual linkages between workfarist activation and quasi-marketisation. It is argued that both are animated by a normative commitment to the commodification of non-employed labour and a shared theory of agency that assumes neither welfare nor administrative subjects can be trusted to work reliably unless externally incentivised to do so.

Chapter Four then examines differences in service delivery between JobPath and LES organisations, both in terms of service-users' experiences and frontline workers' perspectives on the animating values and practice models shaping their delivery of employment services. The evidence reviewed in that chapter establishes conclusively that a more demanding and workfarist model was being delivered at the coalface of JobPath than at the frontline of LES.

Chapter Five zooms out from the micro-level of the caseworker-client interactions to consider the organisational dynamics behind these observed practice differences. Specifically, it identifies two key mechanisms by which quasi-marketisation reshapes agency at the street-level to push policy implementation in a more workfarist direction: the *politics of discretion*, which refers to the disciplinary effects of targets and performance measurement on street-level choice, and the *politics of professionalism*, which describes how marketisation reshapes the kinds of occupational backgrounds, professional identities, and normative beliefs about unemployment that street-level workers bring to their work.

Chapter Six concludes with some reflections on what the Irish case contributes to the broader international understanding of the dynamics between workfare and quasi-marketisation. It also synthesises the findings of the previous chapters to produce a theoretical model of how the commissioning of employment services via instruments of market governance spills over into the production of workfarist policy practices at the micro-level through reshaping street-level agency via politics of professionalism and discretion.

TWO

Welfare reform in post-crisis Ireland

Ireland offers a particularly fascinating case for studying the interplay between the social policy turn towards activation and the governance turn towards marketisation. Until relatively recently, it was very much a latecomer to the contemporary workfare project, but since 2010 it has undergone a period of 'rapid and compressed' reform (Dukelow, 2021: 47). The scale of change has been likened to a 'transformation, not just of policy and processes, but of the entire spirit of welfare' (Boland and Griffin, 2018: 101) in Ireland. The drivers of reform are complex and much debated (see Dukelow, 2015; Murphy, 2016; Hick, 2018). Ireland's financial bailout by the Troika (the International Monetary Fund, European Central Bank, and European Commission) in late 2010 was clearly an important catalyst, as was the threefold increase in the number of people on unemployment payments from 2008 to 2011.

The Troika insisted upon structural welfare reform as a condition of bailout, emphasising especially the need for greater 'conditionality on work and training availability' and stronger 'sanction mechanisms for beneficiaries not complying with job-search conditionality' (European Commission, 2011: 63). This followed on the heels of an OECD review that heavily criticised Ireland's pre-crisis welfare model for allowing people to receive jobseeker payments 'without registration for placement or any other contact with employment services' (Grubb et al, 2009: 5). Nonetheless several key reforms only materialised after Ireland's loan agreement with the Troika had already ended. This reinforces questions about the degree to which the reforms to income supports and employment services institutions reviewed in this chapter involved external 'policy "coercion"' (Hick, 2018: 2) or were more a case of international actors 'pushing against an open door' (Dukelow, 2015). This question of the origins of the reforms is returned to several times, although the main interest lies less in where the reforms came from than in *what* they signified for the trajectory of activation and 'sectoral division of welfare' (Murphy and McGann, 2022: 2) in Ireland.

To appreciate the magnitude of reform over the past decade, it is helpful to first understand the contours of Ireland's pre-crisis welfare state and the activation model that presided during the early 2000s. Accordingly, the chapter begins by briefly reflecting on the pre-crisis period and considering the extent to which Ireland resembled a 'liberal' welfare state. This is followed by a detailed excavation of the changes to income supports that were enacted following the crisis, which saw Ireland's welfare state evolve from 'a predominantly passive system' (J Whelan, 2021: 10) focused on training and job creation into one more and more focused on accelerating job-search conditionality. Yet the success of these reforms would depend on the country's institutional capacity to implement activation. This was far from a given, considering the extensive criticisms – not just from the OECD but also domestic actors – that Ireland's active labour market programmes were 'fragmented, and lacking ambition' (NESC, 2011: xv).

Institutional reform was clearly much needed. As detailed, this took the shape of integrating income and employment supports but also, crucially, outsourcing activation of the long-term unemployed to private providers through the competitive procurement of a new JobPath service. This turn towards market governance has further intensified in recent years, with the country's network of community-delivered LES coming under increased pressure from the DSP to be restructured through competitive procurement and performance-based contracting. Indeed, the publication of this book comes just as Ireland emerges from a second wave of 'creeping marketisation' (Murphy and McGann, 2022: 1) that involved putting *all* externally delivered services out to competitive tender and extending the use of Payment-by-Results to Local Area Employment Services.

Ireland's 'pre-crisis' welfare state

Ireland is often now considered a liberal welfare state (Dukelow and Kennett, 2018) but this has not always been the case. Indeed, positioning the Irish welfare state of the late 1990s and early 2000s within the comparative worlds of welfare capitalism has been described as 'a highly moveable feast' (Cousins, 1997: 226) given the country's 'mix of ideological influences' (Daly and Yeates, 2003: 87) from liberalism, to Catholicism, to colonialism, and nationalism. For instance, where Murphy suggests its broad features 'were largely consistent' (2016: 434) with a liberal regime given the degree of inequality and weakness of labour market regulation, Payne and McCashin (2005) position it as closer to a 'Catholic corporatist' regime. This was due not only to the historical role of the Catholic Church in shaping welfare state development (Cousins, 1997; Daly and Yeates, 2003) but also the presence of strong social partnership institutions incorporating employers, unions, and latterly the community sector in national negotiations on wage regulation and social policy from the late 1980s until 2008.

The main motivation for grouping 'pre-crisis' Ireland as a liberal welfare state was its proximity to Britain, and the fact that its building blocks were a legacy of its colonial past (Cousins, 1997; Daly and Yeates, 2003). However, several features differentiated it from its neighbour and liberal regimes more broadly. During the early 2000s, headline benefit rates were far higher than in the UK (Dukelow and Considine, 2014b), there was minimal use of sanctions (Cousins, 2019), and – most unusually for a liberal regime – there was 'a very high level of welfare state legitimacy' (Payne and Mccashin, 2005: 3) in terms of public support for welfare expenditure. This is not to say that Ireland's pre-crisis welfare state included no demanding elements whatsoever. Claimants *could* be disqualified from benefits for up to nine weeks for various reasons such as not providing 'sufficient evidence of realistic, consistent, or genuine job-search', being dismissed for misconduct, or being deemed to have 'refused' work or training (Grubb et al, 2009: 83–84). In practice, however, job-search monitoring was sporadic at best and employment assistance was not part of the monthly sign-on process but delivered by an institutionally separate national training and employment authority, An Foras Áiseanna Saothair (FÁS).

FÁS was formed in 1987 when Ireland's National Manpower Service merged with the Youth Employment Training Agency and another vocational training agency known as AnCo. It was therefore anchored in a predominant focus on vocational training and governed by a board of management appointed by the Minster for Enterprise, Trade, and Employment rather than the Minister for Social Protection. From the late 1990s, under the National Employment Action Plan (NEAP) that Ireland developed to implement the European Employment Strategy, claimants were to be referred to FÁS for job-search assistance after three months on payments. FÁS would also act as the point of referral for directing claimants to externally delivered programmes such as training courses provided by further education and community colleges; work-experience placements through the Community Employment (CE) programme; job-search training provided by Job Clubs; and more intensive guidance services for the long-term unemployed provided by LES. However, FÁS case officers 'rarely' (Grubb et al, 2009: 95) *mandated* participation in these external programmes as evidenced by the fact that just 66 jobseekers in total were sanctioned between 2004 and 2006 for refusing to participate in activation programmes. Indeed, the overall rate of sanctioning for any reason during this period was estimated at less than 0.79 per cent of claimants per year. In other words, Ireland had 'either the lowest or close to the lowest' (Grubb et al, 2009: 85) rate of sanctioning welfare claimants out of any OECD country. In the words of the OECD's then Director for Employment, Labour, and Social Affairs Ireland's NEAP was like 'the emperor who had no clothes'; it paid lip service to the *idea* of activation but 'there was no implementation of the principles' (Martin, 2015: 9). Indeed, a study by the Economic and Social Research Institute found that referral to FÁS actually reduced claimants' chances of finding employment. The study authors interpreted this through a workfarist lens, attributing the result to claimants' 'lowering their job-search intensity' as they 'gained information on the lack of conditionality, monitoring and sanctions' (McGuinness et al, 2019: 152).

Despite the near absence of sanctions or job-search conditionality, Ireland's spending on active labour market measures was relatively high at 0.64 per cent of gross domestic product (GDP) compared with between 0.35 and 0.39 per cent of GDP in other Anglophone countries (NESC, 2011). It was also focused on a different mix of measures.

Bonoli (2010) classifies activation measures into four ideal types: (i) 'incentive reinforcement' approaches such as time limits on payments, and sanctions for work refusal; (ii) 'employment assistance' programmes such as job-search services; (iii) 'occupation' measures such as public or community work placements; and (iv) 'human capital investment' through education and vocational training. In broad terms, workfare models favour 'incentive reinforcement' and 'employment assistance' measures over human capital investment or occupational measures. However, Ireland's pre-crisis model was characterised by expenditure on 'occupation' and 'human capital investment' measures. In 2006, spending on direct job creation measures (the CE programme) accounted for 0.20 per cent of GDP, the highest out of any OECD country. Spending on training programmes accounted for a further 0.24 per cent of GDP. This was more than double the estimated 0.1 per cent of GDP that the UK and Australia each spent on training measures (OECD, 2022).

In summary, Ireland was a comparatively high spender on activation programmes but lacked a coherent 'overall labour activation framework' (Murphy, 2012: 40). To the extent that it had an activation model, it was 'low-intensity' (NESC, 2011: xv) and more akin to being a human capital rather than workfarist model. Wiggan attributes this to years of 'propitious economic growth' during the Celtic Tiger period, which enabled successive governments to increase expenditure while showing 'little interest' (2015b) in activation. Others point to Ireland's social partnership model, which afforded a series of veto points for unions and community organisations to block politically contested reforms. Inward migration from EU expansion also meant that employers could meet labour shortages by importing labour rather than 'the more difficult challenge of activating reserve domestic labour' (Murphy, 2012: 35).

Austerity and activation

The financial crisis was a watershed for activation policy development in Ireland for both political and fiscal reasons. Policy inertia was no longer an option as the number of people claiming unemployment payments soared along with the country's fiscal deficit. The incidence of very long-term unemployment (lasting two years or more) increased from below 1 per cent in 2007 to 6.4 per cent by early 2011 (Köppe and Maccarthaigh, 2019). This prompted a threefold increase in the number of people on the Live Register, from 158,752 people in January 2007 to a peak of 470,288 claimants in July

2011 (DEASP, 2019). Meanwhile, Ireland's GDP contracted by 14 per cent as the country went from having a small budget surplus to facing the largest budget deficit in the Eurozone (Regan, 2013).

The financial crisis quickly became reframed 'as a debt crisis', the solution to which was presented as a 'politics of austerity' (Dukelow and Considine, 2014a: 59). Faced with a choice between raising taxes and cutting expenditure, Ireland opted decidedly for fiscal consolidation. This was underpinned by the belief that high taxation would undermine any future recovery and that, as the then Minister for Finance argued, Ireland would 'not create jobs by increasing the penalty on work and investment' (Lenihan, 2009). Even before Ireland's loan agreement, all major parties had embraced the need for austerity. A special group was established in 2009 to find fiscal savings through spending cuts, proposing €5.3 billion of budget cuts that included €1.8 billion in cuts to social protection (Hick, 2018: 6).

In December 2010, a coalition government led by Fianna Fáil and the Greens formally signed a Memorandum of Understanding with the Troika to financially bail Ireland out. That government soon lost office, with Fine Gael and Labour winning power and taking responsibility for implementing the terms of Ireland's loan agreement. The Troika's presence coupled with the fact that the agreement was signed by a previous government provided the new government with 'scope for "blame avoidance"' (Hick, 2018: 2) to push through strategies of 'coercive commodification' (Dukelow and Kennett, 2018: 496) that Hick (among others) suggests were essentially domestic in origin.

Written into the bailout terms were obligations to reduce expenditure on social protection by €750m in 2011, along with 'strengthening activation measures' through, among other things, applying 'sanction mechanisms for beneficiaries not complying with job-search conditionality and recommendations for participation in labour market programmes' (European Commission, 2011: 63). Many of these commitments were taken from the recommendations of the OECD's review of Ireland's activation policies, which had called for 'a more *coercive* approach' that, it noted, had 'few active advocates within the social partnership process' (Grubb et al, 2009: 130). However, this 'key institutional veto point' (Murphy, 2016: 438) was removed by the demise of social partnership institutions in 2009. Until that point, successive governments had relied on social dialogue with trade unions, employers, farmers, and subsequently (from the mid-1990s) the community sector to negotiate collective wage agreements and labour market policies on a triannual basis. When the economic crisis deepened, the Fianna Fáil/Green government and the Irish Congress of Trade Unions were unable to reach agreement on wages and the Department of Finance assumed a more unilateral role in policy coordination. This increased even further under the new Fine Gael/Labour Government, which established a centralised Economic Management Council to coordinate the management of the crisis comprised of the Taoiseach (Prime Minister), Tánaiste (Deputy Prime Minister), Minister for Finance, and newly created Minister for Public Expenditure and Reform.

Payment cuts, sanctions, and conditionality

Activation reform initially followed a trajectory of simultaneously reducing the compensatory elements of welfare while intensifying regulatory conditions. A series of rate cuts to all unemployment payments were announced in the 2009 and 2010 budgets. The headline rate of Jobseekers Allowance and Jobseekers Benefit was reduced from €204 to €188 per week (Collins and Murphy, 2016) while the payments of younger jobseekers were cut to just €100 per week for those aged 21 or under (excluding those with dependent children) and to €150 per week for those aged between 22 and 25 years of age (Cousins, 2019). This was justified on the grounds of the relative generosity of welfare in Ireland and a repeating narrative that Ireland 'lived beyond its means' (Dukelow and Considine, 2014b: 421). This was exemplified by the argument of the then Minister for Finance, Brian Lenihan, that cutting payments was critical to 'safeguard the generous system we have' and to encourage young people 'to stay close to the labour market while at the same time providing a rate of payment that compares very well internationally' (Lenihan, 2009).

Ireland progressively reoriented its system towards incentive reinforcement via a three-pronged approach of 'reducing benefit levels, reducing duration of entitlement, and tightening eligibility conditions' (Dukelow, 2021: 50). To this end, the number of contributions that were needed to qualify for unemployment social insurance – the contributory Jobseekers Benefit (JB) – were doubled while the duration that people could remain on JB was reduced to between one and two years.

The use of conditionality was also intensified under the Social Welfare Miscellaneous Provision Act, which came into effect in April 2011. The act introduced new 'penalty rates' in the form of a 25 per cent reduction in payments that could be applied to those on jobseeker payments. While less severe than the nine-week disqualification that previously applied, these penalty rates could be applied in a wider range of circumstances including 'failure to participate in an appropriate employment support scheme, work experience or training' (Cousins, 2019: 32). Moreover, the capacity to levy sanctions in the form of payment reductions rather than payment disqualification also served to make the threat of being sanctioned that bit more palpable. Case officers, presumably, would have less reservations about reducing a person's weekly payment by €44 than they would have about disqualifying someone from payments for up to nine weeks. This appears to be reflected in the data which points to a continuous growth in the number of people penalty rated during the post-crisis years. In 2012, a total of 1,471 claimants were penalty rated. By 2016, this number had reached 9,565 claimants, rising to a total of 12,380 people in 2018 – and despite the overall number of people on the Live Register more than halving during this period (Dáil Éireann, 2019). So, while the overall incidence of sanctioning in Ireland remains modest in international comparative terms, there has been an elevated increase in their use over the past decade.

In early 2012, the benefit cuts and changes to eligibility conditions outlined earlier were consolidated into a formalised activation strategy, *Pathways to Work*. The strategy marked a decided turn towards a more Australian-like mutual obligations model of activation. The government promised substantial institutional reform of employment services so that people would 'no longer remain on the Live Register for lengthy periods without an appropriate offer of assistance from the state' with the flipside being that 'individuals will be made aware of *their responsibility to commit to job-search* and/or other employment, education and training activities or risk losing welfare entitlements' (Government of Ireland, 2012: 5–6, emphasis added). This individualised responsibility would now be formalised in a new welfare contract, the Record of Mutual Commitments, to be entered into at the point of claiming benefits. It would be further documented and updated in Personal Progression Plans (PPPs) that jobseekers would agree with an assigned employment advisor or case manager.

A new statistical profiling tool would also be introduced to assess jobseekers' 'Probability of Exit' (PEX) from unemployment during the first 12 months of their claim. Claimants would complete a profile questionnaire as part of the registration process. Those with a high PEX score would be steered towards self-directed job-search activity for the first three months; those with a mid-point PEX score would be referred for group sessions 'on how to improve their job-search activities'; while those with a low PEX score or who were on payments for 12 months or more would be referred for 'one-to-one support from an experienced employment services advisor' (Government of Ireland, 2012: 12). Initially, this more intensive case management was to be provided either by case officers in the publicly run employment service, or by a mediator in the network of LES that claimants could be referred to by FÁS. However, foreshadowing what was to follow, the strategy signalled the government's intention to implement 'job activation of long-term unemployed' via a privatised implementation structure and on 'a "payment-by-results" basis' (Government of Ireland, 2012: 21).

Widening conditionality

As Ireland's activation model devolved around conditionality and incentive reinforcement, its reach was also extended. *Pathways to Work* tightened the focus on activation into full-time employment. Opportunities for combining benefits with part-time employment became more restricted as claimants in part-time employment became subject to in-work conditionality. Another early proposal was to consolidate all working-age payments into a Single Working-Age Payment that would see the forms of job-search conditionality that were applicable to those on jobseeker payments extended 'to lone parents, partners/spouses, people with disabilities and carers' (Collins and Murphy, 2016: 74).

Ultimately, the attempt to extend conditionality to those on disability or carers payments and to partners – or 'qualified adults' as they are known in the parlance of Ireland's (male) breadwinner model – lost momentum. Successive governments have largely continued to treat welfare dependency as unproblematic *provided* someone is not considered the 'primary' income earner in their household (Murphy, 2018; Dukelow, 2021). Lone parents, by contrast, have not received the same degree of political protection from activation (Collins and Murphy, 2016). Reflecting different 'dynamics of deservingness' (Dukelow, 2021: 56) in Irish social policy, they have been targeted through a series of changes to the eligibility conditions for the One Parent Family Payment which, at the time of the crisis, was payable up until a person's youngest child reached 18 years of age (or 22 if they were in third-level education). Reform of the payment had been on the DSP's agenda since 2006, although there was little political appetite for progressing a reform that was expected to meet with strong opposition from the social partners (Cousins, 2019). This changed following the crisis, as the age at which a lone parent lost entitlement was progressively reduced. Initially, it was proposed that lone parents would migrate to the Jobseekers' Allowance once their youngest child turned seven. However, the community sector successfully mounted a *Seven is Too Young* campaign, leading to the creation of an interim transitional payment for lone parents who whose youngest child was aged between 7 and 14. This payment shielded lone parents from the requirement to seek full-time employment, which only applied when their youngest child reached 14 years of age.

Administrative and governance reform

The upshot of the changes to social security just reviewed has been what Whelan describes as a widening of 'the compulsive geography of the Irish welfare state' (2021: 14). The experience of claiming payments has become characterised by increasing levels of conditionality as Ireland's system of social protection has 'entered a stage of continuing compulsion' (Whelan, 2022: 26). In the process, the problem of unemployment has also become reframed in increasingly individualised terms; as a 'personal failure to be remedied by personal transformation' (Boland and Griffin, 2021: 171) in the form of claimants becoming 'more active in *their efforts* to find work' (Government of Ireland, 2012: 10, emphasis added). Having outlined the key changes in social protection, the remainder of the chapter details the administrative and governance reforms of service delivery organisations that have followed suit. For, as discussed in Chapter One, the march of workfare has as much to do with the reconfiguration of street-level organisations as it has to do with formal shifts in active labour policy.

The death of FÁS

The first major administrative reform was a long-overdue overhaul of the national training and employment authority, FÁS. The state-run employment service had been much criticised for its weak implementation of pre-crisis policy commitments to activation (Grubb et al, 2009; NESC, 2011; McGuinness et al, 2019), and pressure on FÁS intensified when a corporate governance and expenses scandal broke in late 2008 culminating in the resignation of its director (Murphy, 2012; Köppe and MacCarthaigh, 2019). Shortly afterwards, a proposal to merge income and employment supports into a National Employment and Entitlements Service was announced. This integration of benefits and employment supports was standard in other European countries and a core recommendation of the OECD's review (Grubb et al, 2009: 132). It had also been 'a long-standing' (Köppe and MacCarthaigh, 2019: 142) reform ambition in Ireland but one that had hitherto failed to gain any political traction partly due to resistance from public sector unions who opposed merging staff from a semi-autonomous agency and a government department with 'distinct organisational cultures' (NESC, 2011: xxiv).

The newly elected Fine Gael/Labour government was determined to press ahead with the reform, making the integration of all employment and benefit supports into 'a single delivery unit' (Government of Ireland, 2011: 8) under the responsibility of the DSP a core plank of its programme for government. It dissolved FÁS in late 2011, transferring its training functions to 16 new regional Education and Training Boards that were overseen by a new Further Education and Training Authority (SOLAS). The DSP would assume oversight of all employment services, with the approximately 700 employment services staff of FÁS being subsumed into the department along with about a thousand community welfare officers from the Health Service

Executive. The new Intreo service, as it became known, was iteratively rolled out from 2012 along with a more structured case management approach, as envisaged under *Pathways to Work*. The level of support that claimants would now receive would depend on their assessed probability of exiting the Live Register, although early evaluations suggested that many claimants were never actually formally assessed or, if they were, their PEX ratings were often 'not usable' (Kelly et al, 2019: iii) due to missing data. The new employment service would also be underpinned by an information management system known as BOMi (Business Object Model implementation) for recording all client interactions, the details of jobseekers' Personal Progression Plans, and their appointment attendance.

Local Employment Services

The dissolution of FÁS and transfer of its employment services functions to the DSP also had far-reaching ramifications for Ireland's externally delivered employment services, which had previously operated under contract to FÁS. In 2011, these contracted services mainly comprised programmes operated by community organisations:

- *Jobs Clubs* operated by 40 not-for-profit organisations across 43 locations to provide short-term (one to four weeks) job-search assistance and group training primarily for those considered 'job ready';
- *Employability* services for people with a health condition, injury or disability (who participated voluntarily) were delivered by 24 not-for-profit organisations in 31 areas; and
- *LES* operated by 22 not-for-profit organisations (mainly local development companies) across 25 different locations to provide intensive employment guidance to long-term unemployed and other jobseekers considered more distant from employment.

There was 'no formal procurement' (DSP, 2021a: 4) of these community sector delivered services. Rather they were procured through annual rolling contracts on a 'costs-met' basis, with the Irish Government spending approximately €19 million and €5 million per year respectively on LES and Jobs Clubs between 2014 and 2017 (Lavelle and Callaghan, 2018). Of the community sector delivered programmes, LES are the most directly relevant to this book. This is not only because of their comparative size as by far the largest of the community sector delivered employment services but also because they stood in direct competition to JobPath when Ireland's quasi-market in employment services launched in 2015. From mid-2015 until 2022, LES and JobPath providers essentially competed for the same client pool – people on jobseeker payments for 12 months or more, or who had been assessed as being at high risk of long-term unemployment. The presence of JobPath was regarded by the network of LES as a direct threat to their ongoing status in Ireland's mixed economy of activation, prompting the community sector to mount a series of defensive campaigns against marketisation as discussed later in this chapter.

LES have been a feature of Ireland's employment services system for more than 25 years. They were established in 1995 following the recommendations of a National Economic and Social Forum report on long-term unemployment, which called for more intensive and locally based employment services to be provided alongside FÁS in areas with high labour market exclusion. As such, they are intendedly place-based services. This is also reflected in the fact that the vast majority are delivered by local development companies or 'partnerships', many of which also provide other labour market programmes such as Jobs Clubs and the CE programme. These state-funded companies operate on a not-for-profit basis under the governance of boards comprised of elected officials, representatives of statutory bodies, members of community organisations, trade unions, and employers. So, they are closely aligned with Ireland's older social partnership model.

Up until the post-crisis period of welfare reform, LES were anchored in a 'guidance-led' (N Whelan, 2021: 92) and voluntary engagement model focused on the needs of those more distant from the labour market. However, the *Pathways to Work* activation strategy saw a shift in the LES client-base as the bulk of their caseload became jobseekers referred by Intreo for mandatory activation. Whelan observes how the ethos of LES as guidance-led services became 'diluted' by the shift from FÁS to the DSP, and the associated focus on mandatory activation (2021: 92).

Another important change was the introduction of targets and performance measurement as the DSP increasingly sought to steer contractors through instruments of corporate governance. In 2013, LES were set the target of progressing at least 50 per cent of their annual caseload into training or employment. In 2016, this was revised to focus exclusively on job placements and up until 2021 each LES provider had a target of placing at least 30 per cent of its activation clients into 30 or more hours of employment per week (although job sustainment was not measured). This was a blanket target that proved controversial for its failure to take any account of local labour market variation or differences in providers' caseload mix (McGann, 2022a). A review of LES performance conducted on behalf of the DSP found that only half of LES achieved the target in 2016 (INDECON, 2018). The review highlighted the absence of financial penalties for under-performance, criticising the lack of a 'systemic link between funding of the LES and their performance' (INDECON, 2018: xi). It recommended active consideration of a 'competitive procurement model for future provision of services' (INDECON, 2018: xiii), which ultimately eventuated in late 2021 when the DSP announced a request for tender for new Local Area Employment Services – to be partly funded based on Payment-by-Results – that would replace the existing LES and Jobs Clubs contracts.

Enter JobPath

The integration of income support and employment services under Intreo, and changes to how LES were contracted following *Pathways to Work*, undoubtedly constituted major institutional reforms of employment services in Ireland. However, it is arguably the commissioning of JobPath that has been the most far-reaching post-crisis governance reform given the extent to which it marked a decisive turning point towards market governance in the delivery of welfare-to-work.

The contracting of private providers had been flagged in *Pathways to Work*, which cited the UK and Australian examples of 'activation outsourcing' and procuring services based on 'Payment-by-Results' as a model that had 'proven effective' (Government of Ireland, 2012: 21). Nonetheless, the DSP maintained that it was not any philosophical belief in the superiority of marketised implementation structures but sheer practical necessity that dictated the need for outsourcing. The surge in claimant numbers coupled with the policy shift towards active case management had severely stretched existing employment services capacity, with Ireland having a ratio of approximately 1,000 unemployed jobseekers per case manager in 2014 compared to international norms of between 100 and 150 clients per advisor (DEASP, 2019: 8). With a freeze on public sector hiring, the DSP's secretary general argued before a parliamentary committee that the combination of 'direct and contracted resource capacity [was] insufficient to provide a high level of service to all of the people currently on the Live Register' and that procuring additional services from the market was therefore critical 'to cope with a cyclical but diminishing peak in caseload' (cited in Murphy and McGann, 2022: 6).

The procurement of JobPath was formally framed in pragmatic terms as a mechanism to bring onboard additional case management capacity (Wiggan, 2015b). Nonetheless, it was also an 'opportunity in crisis' (Murphy and McGann,

2022: 6) to enact public management reforms that the government had long been considering. The Fine Gael/Labour Government had come to power chastising the 'persistent under-performance' (Government of Ireland, 2011: 28) of Ireland's public sector and promising to 'open up the delivery of public services to a range of providers' and to fund services in new ways so that they are 'less expensive for the taxpayer' (Government of Ireland, 2011: 29–30). The commissioning of JobPath, announced in December 2013, was celebrated by the newly established Department of Public Expenditure and Reform as a model for a future where there would be 'more commissioning' and services would be funded 'based on releasing funds in return for delivering specific outcomes' (DPER, 2014: 15).

The request for tender to deliver the new employment service suggested 'a striking resemblance' (Lowe, 2015: 117) between JobPath and a neighbouring employment services market, Britain's Work Programme. This came as little surprise to Irish social policy observers since the DSP had engaged the UK's Centre for Economic and Social Inclusion to develop JobPath's procurement model. Like the Work Programme, JobPath would follow a 'prime contractor' model. Rather than contracting with tens of providers, the government would instead deal with a select few 'well-capitalised "top tier" providers' (Wiggan, 2015a: 120). These 'primes' would be awarded high-value contracts for large areas but be permitted to subcontract some or all of service provision. This was how the Work Programme then operated: 18 'primes' were contracted by the Department for Work and Pensions (DWP) to manage delivery in the same number of contract package areas (with at least two primes per contract area). But beneath these primes were hundreds of supply chain partners that the DWP had no direct oversight of.

The advantage of this model was that it reduced transaction costs for the purchaser from fewer bids to evaluate, fewer contracts to negotiate, and fewer providers to monitor.

However, the downside was that it placed frontline provision at increased remove from the commissioner, who relied on the primes to manage how contracts were being implemented by their partners. It also limited the 'types of organisations' (Wiggan, 2015b) capable of tendering for contracts due to the financial value but also the geographical size of the contract package areas up for award. This worked to the exclusion of smaller, more specialist providers who may not have had the geographical coverage or financial scale to meet the minimum capital and infrastructure requirements for managing 'prime-sized', performance-based contracts. For instance, to be eligible to bid for JobPath, tenderers were required to have an annual turnover of €20m for the three preceding years (Wiggan, 2015b). Like the Work Programme, JobPath's funding model was also heavily weighted towards Payment-by-Results. Outcome payments comprised more than 90 per cent of the estimated €3,718 in total possible payments that providers could earn, on average, per client (DEASP, 2019: 17). This is an indicative estimate only. The actual value of the payments available to providers was subject to price-bidding during tendering.

Providers also received differentiated payments depending on the duration of full-time employment – 13, 26, 39, or 52 weeks – clients sustained, and the customer group they were in. To incentivise providers to focus on their more disadvantaged clients, JobPath participants were segmented into different customer groups based on their duration of unemployment 'with more challenging clients attracting larger payments' (Lowe, 2015: 121). Again, this differentiated payment model closely mirrored the design of the Work Programme, which offered higher payments if clients were receiving a disability or illness payment rather than a jobseeker's allowance. However, in the case of the Work Programme, the differential pricing model proved ineffective. One key reason was that providers felt that the prices on offer for outcomes with more disadvantaged groups were not high enough to offset the additional costs they predicted they would need to incur to place them into jobs. So, they ignored the higher payments on offer for people in the disability or illness payment customer group and concentrated on easier to place groups (House of Commons, 2015: 22).

The DSP initially invited bids to deliver JobPath in four areas: Border, Midlands, and West (Lot 1); Cork Central, Southeast, and Mid-Leinster (Lot 2); South and Southwest (Lot 3); and Dublin (Lot 4). However, tenderers could combine areas into 'super lots' (Lowe, 2015: 118) as the two successful bidders, Seetec and Turas Nua, did. The two successful bidders also each brought experience of delivering the Work Programme to the Irish market. Seetec, which at the time held Work Prorgamme prime contracts in three areas, was awarded the JobPath contract for Dublin and the Border, Midlands, and West areas. Turas Nua, which was awarded the JobPath contract for all remaining areas, was a joint venture between the Irish cooperative FRS Recruitment and the UK-based Working Links, which delivered the Work Programme in Scotland, Wales, and southwest England.

Each provider had a monopoly in different parts of the country, confining the dynamics of market competition to the tendering stage. This was a significant departure from the UK and Australian markets that had informed JobPath's design, which included multiple providers in each area on the assumption that the innovation and efficiency gains of quasi-market models depended on maintaining competition between 'a sufficiently large number of service providers' (Struyven and Steurs, 2005: 7). For instance, in the Australian model, there are periodic business reallocations from low to high performing providers, meaning that under-performing agencies risk losing their share of clients within a region. There was no such 'post-procurement competition' (Wiggan, 2015b) in Ireland's quasi-market, even if jobseekers could in theory always be redirected to LES as an alternative to JobPath. One rationale for contracting only one provider per region was the need to create a stable market. The DSP was concerned that a multi-provider model would make the contract less attractive to bidders, particularly in the low-density areas outside Dublin. It would also pose challenges for ensuring the volume of referrals needed to make the contract profitable.

A further point of departure from the Work Programme contract model was JobPath's 'grey-box' design. Minimum standards concerning both the content and frequency of services were specified in detail. Employment offices would have to be located no more than one hour by public transport from where clients lived. Providers would also be required to conduct a one-on-one appointment with each client within 20 days of referral, and to maintain monthly meetings thereafter. Other minimum requirements included drawing up a PPP for each client at the first meeting and reviewing this quarterly. Caseload sizes were also capped at 120 jobseekers per advisor and were to be enforced through periodic inspections of contractors' offices coupled with monthly meetings between the DSP and the two contractors to review their performance and compliance (Roche and Griffin, 2022). To further incentivise a focus on quality, customer satisfaction surveys would be conducted at least annually. This focus on service-users' experiences was written into the contract, along with a clause allowing the DSP to reclaim up to 15 per cent of contractors' payments if they were evaluated poorly by service-users.

For these reasons, JobPath can best be described as falling somewhere between a state-managed and provider-directed quasi-market. Since its commencement in mid-2015, the state has substantially ceded control over the delivery of welfare-to-work to private companies – commoditising claimants in a way that they had hitherto been shielded from in Ireland (see Chapter Three). Yet private agencies have not been given the same free rein over service delivery that they have enjoyed in other liberal welfare states; most notably during the early years of Australia's Job Network (1998–2003) and under Britain's Work Programme which were both 'black box' designs characterised by a 'hands-off' approach to regulating implementation.

Creeping marketisation

JobPath marked a major turning point in the governance of employment services in Ireland. It has been likened to a process of 'privatisation by stealth' (Murphy and Hearne, 2019: 457) in that it was introduced without much public debate and with far-reaching implications for the sectoral division of welfare. It has seen Ireland's employment services landscape evolve from a two-tiered to a three-tiered mixed economy of activation that is now firmly underpinned by market governance. The impact on community sector providers was immediately felt in terms of a sharp decline in client referrals, from 71,424 activation referrals to LES in 2015 to just 39,984 in 2017 (Lavelle and Callaghan, 2018).

The marketisation logic underpinning JobPath has increasingly come to be viewed as a threat to the model of local, not-for-profit provision that predominated during the late 1990s and early 2000s. Several motions have been brought before the Dáil (Ireland's lower house) calling for the government to roll back the marketisation of employment services. The first of these was in February 2019, when Sinn Féin representatives successfully brought a motion calling for the DSP to 'immediately cease all referrals to the JobPath service' and to 'end the use of "payment-by-results" models in job activation schemes' (Dáil Éireann, 2019a). This followed a series of hearings and submissions to an Oireachtas (Parliamentary) Committee on Employment Affairs and Social Protection that were highly critical of JobPath's funding model and ethos (see Murphy and McGann, 2022).

In late 2021, JobPath again came under sustained criticism from two Oireachtas committees. The Joint Committee on Social Protection, Community and Rural Development, and the Islands questioned its public benefit, when a total of €252 million had been spent on the programme from July 2015 to July 2021 to yield only 70,740 job placements (out of 376,964 referrals) of which just 24,000 had lasted 52 weeks or more. The committee argued that a '7 per cent job sustainment rate does not represent value-for-money and is indicative that outcomes-based payment models do not provide long-term benefits for those seeking employment' (Oireachtas Committee, 2021: 8). This criticism of JobPath was echoed by the Public Accounts Committee, which called for future programmes to be managed 'by either the Department or community-based organisations' and for contractors to be chosen 'based on broader criteria than simply cost' (PAC, 2021: 4). This was a reference to the fact that the DSP had defended JobPath on grounds of cost, claiming that the average fee paid per participant was just €873 compared with €1,052 per LES participant (PAC, 2021: 4).

The context for these criticisms was the DSP's decision to submit all externally delivered services to a second wave of competitive procurement from mid-2021. This included not just JobPath (which was due for re-procurement) but also LES and Jobs Clubs, which had not previously been subject to any form of competitive procurement in what the DSP argued contravened 'good governance and public procurement practice' (DSP, 2021a: 4). The competitive procurement of these latter programmes was first mooted in late 2018, when the then Minister for Social Protection informed the CEOs of partnership companies that the government was seeking to introduce open competition for the existing Jobs Clubs and LES contracts. The DSP subsequently repeatedly stated that it received advice from the Attorney General's office that it was legally required to competitively procure any further external services.

In 2019, the UK-based Institute for Employment Studies and Social Finance Foundation were engaged to advise on the procurement and design of all externally delivered employment services. They recommended a model of staged referral to different services based on participants' duration of unemployment. Intreo would continue to provide employment services during claimants' first year on payments. Following this, claimants would be referred to an externally delivered National Employment Service along the lines of JobPath. After 24 months on payments, claimants would be referred to what has subsequently become termed Regional or Local Area Employment Services.

The COVID pandemic ultimately disrupted these plans to place Ireland's externally delivered employment services 'on a proper contractual footing' (DSP, 2021a: 4). In June 2020, all existing contracts were extended for a further two years in anticipation of a pandemic surge in demand for activation. However, in May 2021, the DSP took its first step towards wider system change when it announced a request for tender for four new Regional Employment Services. These services would be delivered in counties then under-serviced by Jobs Clubs or LES, including Donegal, Sligo, Leitrim, Laois, Offaly, Longford, and Westmeath. This was to foreshadow a country-wide procurement of Local Area Employment Services announced in late 2021. It accompanied the release of an updated *Pathways to Work 2021–25* strategy, which committed to expanding the caseload capacity of employment services by 100,000 jobseekers per annum and reducing the rate of long-term unemployment to 2.5 per cent by 2025 (Government of Ireland, 2021).

In questioning before the Oireachtas, the Minister maintained that the DSP was not looking to privatise employment services nor was the contract model 'a for-profit driven agenda by any manner or means' (Select Committee, 2021). Nonetheless, the request for tender indicated an extension of market governance in that outcome payments – for placing participants into 17 weeks or more of full-time employment – would now constitute 37 per cent of the total potential payments per client. The remaining payments would be comprised of a service start fee (33 per cent) and a fee for completing job plans (30 per cent)

(DSP, 2021b), although the exact fee amounts would depend on tenderers' price bids. So, although the payment model was not as heavily oriented towards Payment-by-Results as the JobPath contract, similar market governance instruments of competitive tendering, price-bidding, and performance-based contracting were in play to the fury of partnership companies.

A defensive campaign was mounted to preserve community-based employment services, including strike action by LES staff and political interventions by Dublin's Lord Mayor and a coalition of Teachtaí Dála (TDs), or Irish members of parliament. In November 2021, a motion was also brought before the Dáil calling for the government to 'protect the not-for-profit and community-based ethos of employment services' and to 'suspend all plans to tender out employment services' (Dáil Éireann, 2021). These campaigns ultimately came to no avail and on 23 December 2021 the DSP issued another request for tender for 17 additional Local Area Employment Services contracts on top of the four Regional Employment Services contracts already being procured. The results of that earlier tender were announced just weeks later, with Seetec and Turas Nua each winning contracts to deliver the new services in Longford/Westmeath and Laois/Offaly respectively.

The procurement of Local Area Employment Services was closely based on the DSP's procurement of Regional Employment Services, being essentially the same programme in different counties. Price-bidding was actively encouraged, and outcome payments comprised a similar proportion (37 per cent) of the total possible payments per client. Despite this market governance approach and rumours that major multinational providers such as Maximus were preparing bids (Power, 2022), virtually all existing LES providers managed to win contracts to deliver the new Local Area Employment Services until mid-2025 (DSP, 2022a). For now, this component of Ireland's mixed economy of activation remains largely in the hands of community sector providers. However, the award of parallel Regional Employment Services contracts to Seetec and Turas

Nua means that community sector providers now face even stiffer competition from these private providers than before. They are delivering essentially the same contract in different counties and will be well positioned to bid for any future Local Area Employment Services contracts.

Re-procurement of the JobPath programme also commenced in mid-2022 in the form of a request for tender to deliver new National Employment Service contracts. The payment model has been refined to focus on four different customer groups and different durations of job sustainment (17, 34, and 52 weeks). However, otherwise the programme represents a continuation of the JobPath model albeit at a smaller scale with contracts estimated to be worth €23.8 million per year compared to the approximately €50 million per year initially spent on JobPath (Lavelle and Callaghan, 2018). This reflects the decline in the numbers on jobseeker payments compared with when JobPath was introduced, and the proposed National Employment Service encompasses a very similar 'grey-box' design. Outcome payments also comprise 90 per cent of the total possible payments per participant that providers can earn (DSP, 2022b), reflecting a continuation of the DSP's commitment to outcomes-based contracting.

By mid-October 2022, the results of the National Employment Service tender had yet to be made public. Although it would be surprising if Seetec and Turas Nua did not win the contracts given the request for tenders was issued only seven weeks before the tender deadline and two of the three contract lots mirrored the areas where Seetec delivered JobPath (Dublin; Connacht, Ulster, and North Leinster) while the third aligned with where Turas Nua delivered JobPath (Munster and South Leinster).

As evident from this overview, the use of market governance instruments to procure employment services and to govern the street-level delivery of welfare-to-work has evolved to become a cornerstone of welfare modernisation in Ireland. Initially this was through institutional layering whereby quasi-marketisation coexisted alongside state-run services and other employment services delivered by community sector providers through annual block grant funding. However, subsequent and more recent governance reforms have seen quasi-marketisation in the form of competitive tendering and performance-based contracting become the default mode for commissioning employment services in Ireland. What was introduced under the pretence of needing to rapidly boost employment services capacity in the short term to cope with a crisis-induced surge in long-term unemployment has become a long-term strategy for governing the delivery of welfare-to-work.

The chapters that follow explore empirically how this turn towards marketisation reshapes the delivery of employment services in form and content, and the extent to which it has accelerated the workfarist turn in Irish social policy as part of a strategy of 'double activation'. It is to this concept, and the underlying empirical research, that the book now turns.

THREE

Exploring double activation

Ireland's recent history of welfare reform, as discussed in Chapter Two, is a timely illustration of how the social policy turn towards activation and the administrative turn towards market governance unfold 'as two sides of a single political project' (Soss et al, 2013: 139). In this case of Ireland, the project was one of moving from a purportedly 'passive' model of welfare to one concerned with catalysing employment through 'job activation of [the] long-term unemployed' (Government of Ireland, 2012: 21). To achieve this, policymakers turned not only to legislative instruments of conditionality (payment penalties). The street-level organisations tasked with implementing *Pathways to Work* were also fundamentally reconfigured. The state-run employment service was replaced with an integrated benefits and employment service (Intreo); LES delivered by not-for-profit organisations became subject to tighter performance measurement and monitoring under a different commissioner (the DSP rather than FÁS); and a Payment-by-Results quasi-market (JobPath) was introduced to bolster institutional capacity.

Initially a pragmatic means to bring additional case managers online amidst a temporary surge in long-term unemployment, the market governance instruments of competitive tendering, price-competition, and performance-based contracting have since evolved to become the default mechanisms for steering welfare-to-work delivery in Ireland. Put simply, Ireland has followed a well-trodden path of extending the project of welfare reform beyond the activation of claimants to the 'double' (Considine et al, 2015: 29; McGann, 2021) or even 'triple'[1] (van Berkel, 2013) activation of the organisations and frontline workers responsible for implementing active labour market policies on the ground.

This chapter takes a closer look at 'double activation' as an analytical lens, and why the concept holds significance beyond describing the conjunction between the two tracks of welfare reform. What is it about the parallel unfolding of governance reforms of delivery organisations that is of wider interest to the shape of activation reform? The chapter also introduces the *GAII* study underpinning this book: the research design and how the study differed from previous studies of the impacts of marketisation on the frontline delivery of employment services. The chapter concludes with a consideration of the underlying conceptual linkages between workfare and marketisation, drawing attention to the theories of motivation they share and the ways in which they each involve a normative commitment to the commodification of claimants. Recognising these points of normative and conceptual intersection helps to elucidate why the two reform tracks work in concert, as further examined in Chapter Four.

'Double activation' as an analytical lens

At one level, the concept of 'double activation' can be approached as a purely descriptive label signifying how 'welfare reform has initiated a tougher regime of social control, not just for welfare clients, but also for their case managers' (Soss et al, 2011a: 230). Just as train tracks proceed in parallel, governance reforms of administrative institutions have followed where substantive changes in social security policy have gone. But why does this matter? Why should we be concerned about attempts to steer delivery organisations through contractualisation and financial incentives above and beyond attempts to discipline the behaviour of claimants? One important reason concerns how governance reforms involve changes in the professional boundaries and organisational conditions in which policy delivery is embedded.

As outlined in Chapter One, the exercise of discretion by street-level workers plays a key role in transposing policy into practice. 'Transposing' is a deliberate choice of term, emphasising that frontline workers do not implement policies straightforwardly. Their actions involve elements of policy*making* as they determine what to do about complex situated cases that aren't fully covered under guidelines. Quasi-market reforms invariably remodel this street-level agency in important ways. First, they involve relocating discretion from bureaucrats in state agencies to case managers employed by private or not-for-profit organisations. In so doing, they not only change the types of organisations employing case managers and other frontline workers. They also potentially change *the types of workers* who are hired to enact policy with citizens.

The workforces of the public, private and community sectors are far from synonymous. Even in similar fields such as education, those working in the different sectors will vary along characteristics such as rates of union membership, qualification, and experience levels. They may also have quite different attitudinal dispositions relevant 'to the shaping of service provision' (Sadeghi and Fekjær, 2018: 78), such as their beliefs about social security or the nature of unemployment. To this extent, a long-standing concern about quasi-markets in employment services is their potential to produce a 'disorganisation of employment relations' (Greer et al, 2017: 109) at the frontline. For example, by eroding rates of union membership and bonds of solidarity between workers and resulting in workers being employed on less secure contracts and hired on the basis of their relative low-cost rather than professional expertise. The latter is an especially important concern considering the multitude of studies documenting the de-skilling of frontline workers following episodes of quasi-marketisation (Considine and Lewis, 2010; Schram, 2012; Greer et al, 2017), and ongoing debates about the importance of 'professionalism' in activation work.

Chapter Five considers these issues in greater detail, including the extent to which activation work constitutes a form of 'professional' practice. Nevertheless, there are important reasons for thinking that the delivery of employment services to people with complex employment-related needs '*should* be organised and managed as professional work' (van Berkel et al, 2021: 2), and that this possibility is being undermined by processes of quasi-marketisation. Put simply, one important way that governance reforms remodel agency is by changing *who holds discretion in policy implementation* and the professional identities, occupational backgrounds, and worldviews informing its use.

A second way that governance reforms remodel discretion is by restructuring the organisational environments in which policy implementation is embedded through the application of managerialist systems of performance measurement. These systems of managerial scrutiny and performance monitoring aim to render frontline decision-making more visible and accountable to specified goals, but they discipline discretion through changing what Brodkin terms 'the calculus of street-level choice' (2011: i259). This is because performance monitoring does more than measure what workers already, or would otherwise, do. It also cultivates different 'habits of mind' (Soss et al, 2011a: 208) such as a relentless focus on meeting 'targets and organisational needs' (van Berkel and Knies, 2016: 64) in response to the number of job placements achieved by individual staff becoming a focus of intensive organisational monitoring. The result may be a focus on 'speed-over-need' (Brodkin, 2011: i266), working to place clients into jobs as rapidly as possible rather than taking the time to build employability through training with a view to more sustained progressions.

The significance of 'double activation' as an analytical lens therefore goes beyond its value as a descriptive label for capturing the convergence between the social policy and administrative tracks of contemporary welfare reform. Rather, it's critical potential lies in tying these reform tracks together to understand 'how efforts to discipline service providers shape efforts to discipline welfare recipients' (Soss et al, 2011a: 209). In other words, how does configuring the delivery of employment services using processes of competitive tendering and performance-based contracting *change* the way that welfare recipients experience and are targeted for activation? Can we isolate the effects of marketisation on street-level delivery beyond the formal changes in activation policies that accompany such administrative reforms?

The GAII study

Behind this book is an empirical study of Ireland's 'mixed economy' activation, and the 'pluri-governance' (McGann, 2022b: 942) approach to employment services commissioning that operated from 2015–2022, when two parallel programmes operating within the same policy space and time were procured through different governance modes. This is distinct from forms of 'hybrid governance' where different modes of governance are threaded together to form an overarching framework that is 'hybrid in nature' (Benish and Mattei, 2020: 282) but which steers all programme delivery within a given administrative field. Ireland's mixed economy of activation was coordinated not by 'hybrid' but by 'pluri' governance. Employment services programmes that were otherwise functionally similar were coordinated via discrete governance modes. In the case of JobPath, market governance instruments of competitive tendering, outcomes-based payment models, and price competition were the central coordinating mechanisms. LES, by contrast, were commissioned predominantly through closed contracting and procedural accountability for inputs ('costs-met' funding). Although targets and performance measurement were increasingly used by the DSP to steer the delivery of LES, providers' funding was not tied to their performance in the way that it was for the JobPath providers. Another potentially important difference between the two programmes is the fact that JobPath was delivered by private firms whereas LES were delivered by place-placed not-for-profit and community development organisations. However, besides these differences in how they were commissioned, the two employment services programmes otherwise coalesced in policy time and space. Both were targeted towards claimants who were long-term unemployed or deemed at 'high risk' of becoming long-term unemployed; and they each operated under the same *Pathways to Work* activation policy setting, with its emphasis on job-search conditionality, the completion of PPPs, and threat of sanctions.

There have been multiple previous studies of quasi-market reforms and their impact on frontline delivery (see especially Bredgaard and Larsen, 2007; Considine et al, 2015; Greer et al, 2017; O'Sullivan et al, 2021). This book builds upon this important body of work. Nevertheless, few studies have been able to *synchronously* compare frontline delivery under different governance conditions, and where alternative instruments coordinate delivery in the same policy field at the same time. The uniqueness of the GAII study lies in how it leveraged the degree of administrative overlap between JobPath and LES to pursue synchronous comparative research on the intersection between workfare and marketisation. It did so through a multi-pronged, mixed-methods approach involving (i) survey and interview research with frontline delivery staff, (ii) interview research with key policy practitioners (civil servants, government advisors) and other stakeholders (executive managers of contracted providers), and (iii) in-depth interviews with service-users about their experiences of participating in welfare-to-work programmes. This enabled data to be triangulated from different sources to enhance the robustness of the findings, with the total dataset comprising 64 in-depth interviews gathered over three waves of qualitative research and 189 survey responses from frontline staff as further outlined next.

Frontline workers

Core to street-level research is a focus on 'opening up the "black box" of policy implementation' (Caswell et al, 2017: 1). Researchers use a range of methods to do so, of which observational fieldwork is among the most powerful (Zacka, 2017; O'Sullivan et al, 2021). This is for its capacity to provide 'a window into actual service encounters as they happen' (O'Sullivan et al, 2021: 58), and to expose areas of 'behaviour that are harder, if not impossible, to reach by other means' (Brodkin, 2017: 133). Direct observation of JobPath and LES staff was however not possible because the fellowship that supported data collection was from January 2020 to December 2021. Ireland, like most other countries, was grappling with the COVID pandemic for much of this period. In-person appointments were effectively suspended, although contracted employment services did continue to operate remotely via telephone or online appointments. So, the method relied upon was a combination of survey research and in-depth interviews with frontline staff.

The research approach facilitated questioning JobPath and LES frontline staff about programme delivery in more typical times, outside the pandemic, which was an extensive focus of both the survey and interview research. Nevertheless, it must be acknowledged that relying on workers' self-reports to illuminate how they use their discretion has its limitations; not least because participants may tell researchers what they think researchers want to hear rather than what they actually do (Jerolmack and Khan, 2014). To some extent, the study's mixed–methods approach mitigated this risk in that the frontline research data could be triangulated against data from other sources to check the veracity of what JobPath and LES staff reported.

The survey research was undertaken from 1 July to 14 August 2020. A total of 189 frontline staff completed the survey, including 77 JobPath staff and 112 LES staff. This may seem a small number of respondents, although it reflects the scale of contracted out provision in Ireland rather than a low response rate. Across the country in 2020, there were only 170 mediators (as advisors are known in LES) working in the LES. Based on the estimates provided by Seetec and Turas Nua, the JobPath providers only employed approximately 253 advisors between them. So, the response rate varied from 30 to 65 per cent.

For the purposes of the survey, frontline staff were defined as employees who work directly with jobseekers to find employment as part of their jobs. As shown in Table 3.1, this predominantly included employment advisors or mediators although it also included some site managers and staff whose job it was to broker placements with employers. Both JobPath providers participated in the survey, as did the network of 22 LES organisations, with senior managers in those organisations circulating details about the study to all their staff and inviting them to participate in the online survey. Consequently, the organisational coverage of the survey is very broad. Further details of the survey sample such as the age, gender, and qualification levels of respondents are reported in Chapter Five, which examines in-depth the differences between the two frontline workforces.

The survey data were analysed using SPSS software, with variations in response tested for statistical significance at the 5 per cent level. The Mann–Whitney U-test (a nonparametric equivalent to the independent samples t-test) was used in cases where the dependent variables were continuous. This allowed for testing the significance of observed differences in the dependent variable for JobPath and LES staff even though data were often asymmetrically distributed. For ordinal dependent variables, Fisher's exact test of independent was principally used due to the small number of responses on some items which precluded the use of the chi-square test.

The survey questionnaire along with the full dataset of responses is available open access via the Zenodo repository (see https://doi.org/10.5281/zenodo.5513839). Altogether, respondents were asked approximately 60 questions about various aspects of how they did their jobs, the extent to which their performance was measured by their employer, what they saw as the priorities when working with jobseekers, and about their own occupational backgrounds and attitudes towards welfare and unemployment. The questionnaire was developed from that used by Considine and colleagues in their successive studies of the frontline delivery of employment services in Australia, the UK, and the Netherlands (Considine, 2001; Considine et al, 2015). The most recent iteration of that work was in 2016, when more than 1,200 Jobactive staff in Australia and several hundred Work Programme staff in the UK were surveyed about their agency practices and personal approaches to delivering welfare-to-work (Considine et al, 2020b; McGann et al, 2020). A particular advantage of this approach in the context of studying Ireland's mixed economy of activation is that it offers the potential not only to compare internal differences between marketised and non-marketised service provision in Ireland but also to compare the Irish quasi-market to its UK and Australian counterparts.

Following the survey, 20 respondents were interviewed in-depth between October 2020 and January 2021. These interviews were conducted via phone and Microsoft Teams to explore early findings from the survey data in greater depth, including how JobPath and LES staff viewed activation and the managerial regimes and systems of performance measurement they worked under. The interview sample was evenly balanced between JobPath and LES staff (see Table 3.1). It included employees from both JobPath agencies and eight different

Table 3.1: Frontline research participants by gender, job role, and location

	Survey respondents		Interviewees	
	JobPath (n = 77)	LES (n = 112)	JobPath (n = 10)	LES staff (n = 10)
Gender				
• Male	25	22	2	1
• Female	52	88	8	9
• Undisclosed or missing	0	2	0	0
Job role				
• Advisor/mediator/case manager	50	89	6	8
• Employer liaison/broker	10	1	2	
• Manager	15	8	2	2
• Receptionist	1	8		
• Other	1	6		
Locations (counties)	N/A	N/A	Dublin, Louth, Offaly, Wicklow, Kildare	Dublin, Louth, Monaghan, Wicklow, Kildare, Limerick, Cork

LES organisations, as well as a mix of advisors/mediators, site managers, and staff who worked as employer liaisons. Most of the managers and employer liaisons had also previously worked as advisors and could therefore discuss their experience of working in a case management role.

Policy practitioners

Besides the frontline interviews, further interviews with nine key stakeholders and policy practitioners were conducted at various intervals. These interviews focused on the commissioning process and the dynamics between the DSP and its contractors; exploring issues around contract design, the funding model, and the performance framework used to steer employment services. The interviewees included an official from the administrative unit of the DSP overseeing employment services contracting, an independent researcher/ consultant who advised the government during the *Pathways to Work* reforms, a senior JobPath executive, five LES coordinators responsible for organising regional networks of LES managers, and a union official representing employment services staff.

Service-users

The final wave of research involved in-depth interviews with 35 former and current service-users about their experiences of welfare-to-work programmes. These interviews were conducted by phone between April and August 2021, following the completion of the research with frontline staff. Consequently, the interviews explored service-users' perspectives on, and experiences of, similarities and discontinuities between JobPath and LES that were observed in data from the research with frontline staff. This included exploring what un(der)employed people found helpful or unhelpful about the nature of the support they received from different providers; the extent to which they were referred to job vacancies, training, or work experience programmes; how their experience of contracted employment services compared with the support they received from Intreo; and whether they felt treated with dignity and respect by providers and frontline staff.

Service-users were recruited for interview in several ways, including via the Twitter and Facebook accounts of Maynooth University's Social Sciences Institute and online discussion fora for jobseekers. The Irish National Organisation of the Unemployed – a federation of community groups, trade unions, welfare rights centres, and unemployed people that is officially recognised by the DSP – also assisted in promoting the research via social media and email distribution lists. Additionally, parallel services used by jobseekers such as Money Advice and Budgeting Services and Adult and Further Education colleges were approached to advertise the research to any of their clients with experience of JobPath or LES.

A purposive sampling approach was used to ensure that the interviewees captured varied experiences by age, gender, and location. As shown in Table 3.2, interviewees came from a broad range of age groups as well as different parts of the country. This was to ensure that the sample captured a balance of service-users across *different* providers. A limitation of previous qualitative studies of people's experiences of JobPath is that they are focused almost entirely on people's experiences of services delivered by Turas Nua (Finn, 2021; J Whelan, 2021; Boland et al, 2022; Whelan, 2022). This stems from the locations of that research (Cork, Waterford, Wexford, and Kildare) which are all counties where Turas Nua is the only JobPath provider. This body of work has been vital in giving voice to the perspectives of the people most impacted by welfare reforms, but it only offers a partial picture. To address this, the JobPath service-users interviewed for the present study were almost evenly balanced between people who had been clients of Turas Nua (15 interviewees) and people with experience of Seetec (16 interviewees). Ten interviewees were former or current clients of LES, including six who had experience of *both* JobPath and LES.

As shown in Table 3.2, most service-users were former clients rather than jobseekers at the time of being interviewed. Indeed, only 11 interviewees were clients of employment services at the time of being interviewed, although in the bulk of cases people's most recent experience of employment services was within the previous 24 months. One important reason for interviewing former clients was so that the study could explore people's experiences before COVID-19, when meetings with advisors were still face-to-face and payment penalties (which

Table 3.2: Profile of service-user interviewees

	Female (n = 19)	Male (n = 16)
Age		
• Under 30 years		2
• 0–39 years	8	3
• 40–49 years	3	5
• 50–59 years	7	4
• 60+ years	1	2
Most recent experience of activation		
• Participating at interview	6	5
• 2018–20	9	8
• Before 2018	4	3
Participated in		
• JobPath:	16	15
◦ Once	10	6
◦ Twice	3	6
◦ Three times or more	3	3
• Local Employment Services	5	5
Location		
• Border (Cavan, Monaghan, Leitrim, Louth, Sligo)	4	1
• Dublin	7	5
• South Leinster (Laois, Offaly, Kildare, Kilkenny, Wicklow)	5	2
• Munster (Cork, Clare, Limerick, Waterford, Tipperary)	3	8

were suspended in March 2020) were still in force. Were the interviews restricted to only people who were participating in employment services at the time of the interview, this would have produced a very a-typical understanding of people's lived-experiences of welfare-to-work.

Notwithstanding the attempt to ensure that the interview sample included a broad range of perspectives by age, gender, and location, there is always the danger of selection bias in research of this nature. Often, the people most likely to volunteer to be interviewed will be those with grievances to report. This can skew the data towards negative assessments of employment services. Hence the importance of triangulating data from different sources, as the GAII study enables through its multi-pronged and mixed-methods approach to data collection.

All interviews were fully transcribed, and a copy of the de-identified transcript (all names used are pseudonyms) was provided to participants for verification. The transcripts were then coded, using NVivo software to help organise the coding of the data, and based on a framework analysis approach (Gale et al, 2013). This relies on consistently coding cases according to pre-defined codes drawn from the literature and emergent recurring themes (and continuously checking previously coded transcripts against emergent themes). Cases (interviewees) are then grouped by variables of interest – for instance, the type of employment service interviewees participated in or worked for – and systematically compared across relevant themes to identify commonalities and differences across groups of cases.

Intersects between workfare and marketisation

Drawing on the GAII study, subsequent chapters consider in detail the practical effects of when workfare meets marketisation. This is in terms of how a marketised implementation structure changes:

1. the balance between the enabling and demanding elements of activation, as examined in Chapter Four;
2. the professional, organisational, and managerial contexts in which the delivery of welfare-to-work is embedded; and

3. the occupational backgrounds and professional identities that street-level workers bring to their work, as discussed in Chapter Five.

Before proceeding with that analysis, it is worth pausing to consider some of the key conceptual features that workfare and marketisation share in common. These include a mutual orientation towards the commodification of non-employed labour and the presumption of a shared theory of motivation that emphasises the 'bad agency' (Wright, 2012: 310) of welfare recipients and street-level workers. Unpacking these conceptual symmetries sheds important light on the symbiosis between workfare and marketisation as 'two sides of the same coin' (van Berkel and van der Aa, 2005: 330).

Commodification

One basic feature that workfare and marketisation share is the commodification of claimants' labour in the sense of treating it as a fungible resource to be extracted for profit. This commodification of non-employed labour is the stated objective of workfarist activation but also the foundational logic of quasi-marketisation (Grover, 2009; McGann, 2021; O'Sullivan et al, 2021), operating as the doxa of contemporary welfare reform. Non-employed labour exists to be traded on the market. Not to do so is to be a dependent, 'free-riding' on the labour of others, whereas the path to independence lies in gainful employment. Hence the proclamation of the then Taoiseach, Enda Kenny, when launching the second iteration of *Pathways to Work* (2016–2020) that he wanted 'to see people independent in work, not dependent on welfare' because 'a job is the best route out of poverty' (DEASP, 2016).

Whether jobs are synonymous with routes out of poverty is of course a matter of some dispute (Patrick, 2012; Seikel and Spannagel, 2018). It might be true in aggregate terms, but it is also the case that activation policies shape labour market conditions in highly salient ways that influence the quality of the available employment pathways (Dean, 2012; Greer, 2016; Raffass, 2016). It is important to recognise that 'activation is part of the framework that gives rise to certain labour market forms rather than just being a response to labour market conditions' (Fuertes et al, 2021: 434). There has been a lively debate in the Irish context over whether post-crisis reforms have intensified rates of low-pay and in-work poverty (see Murphy, 2016; Collins and Murphy, 2021; Dukelow, 2021). The country has one of the highest incidences of low pay in the OECD, with close to a quarter of full-time workers classified as low paid (Collins and Murphy, 2021), meaning that their annual income is less than two-thirds of median annual income.

This debate concerning the intersection between activation and Ireland's low-pay economy reflects a long-standing concern that workfarist policies are less concerned with 'creating jobs for people who don't have them' than with 'creating workers for jobs that nobody wants' (Peck, 2001: 6). To put it provocatively, workfare is not about employment inclusion but about 'pimping the precariat' (Dean, 2012: 358). The argument here is that demanding activation works to exploit labour 'as a disposable commodity available at a discount' (Dean, 2012: 358). Grover goes so far as to argue that the 'ratcheting up' of conditionality inherent to workfare constitutes a regime of 'violent proletarianisation' whereby the prospect of 'immiseration' is structurally deployed to force people 'to commodify their labour power' (2019: 350).

This critique of the political economy of workfare draws on Esping-Andersen's typology of the worlds of welfare capitalism, which differentiates between 'worlds of welfare' according to the extent to which different regimes allow citizens to subsist independently of the market. From this perspective, the post-war era was a heyday of de-commodification. Enhanced benefits in terms of coverage and value coupled with investment in public services provided a substitute for wages and services that would otherwise have to be purchased. Access to social security provided scope for workers to refuse, without pain of starvation, employment that was poorly paid. This is less and less possible due to the enforcement of conduct conditions that 'ratchet up' (Greer, 2016: 169) the pressure on claimants to join what critical political economists, following Marx, term the reserve army of labour; the surplus population of non-employed workers that serves as a readily available supply 'for the lower end of the labour market' (Peck and Theodore, 2000: 123). The size and material conditions of this reserve army shape the degree to which employers can extract profit from acquiring labour. Workfare policies reinforce the reserve army mechanism by threatening the withdrawal of benefits as punishment for 'resistance to low-quality employment' (Raffass, 2017: 354). Labour market competition thus becomes more intensified, enabling wages and conditions to be eroded.

Participants interviewed for this book were acutely aware of this political economy of workfare. Several eloquently articulated how the intensification of job-search conditionality under *Pathways to Work* serviced employers with a fungible supply of workers for low-paid jobs, questioning "what the hell these activation things are about anyway" other than "forming people to put them into a private industry that a lot of the time is highly exploitative" (Frank, service-user, 50s, Clare). As Frank elaborated: "All we are doing is creating that conveyor belt of willing workers, and when they're finished with, they are thrown back on the scrap heap and reshaped and put into something new that needs more human staffing."

The cycle of 'low pay, no pay' was likewise reflected upon by another former service-user who questioned "the thing of where you just find a job [and] there's nothing about job satisfaction or the right job for you". Ultimately, in her experience, it leads "people to take jobs that they don't like, and they end up back on social welfare anyway because they're not happy in their roles and their demoralised" (Claire, service-user, 50s, Dublin).

A vivid example was provided by one interviewee, Aisling, who recounted how she "literally took the worst job possible" working in a hospitality job "that didn't pay minimum wage, didn't have breaks, didn't have a contract" just so she could "get away from JobPath" and the 'ritualised humiliation' (Charlesworth, 2000, cited in Wright et al, 2020: 284) of being forced to attend what she likened to "poverty class" (Aisling, service-user, Dublin, 30s). In another example, a single mother recounted feeling "bullied and harassed" into a junior store assistant role in an off license just "to keep them off my back". She described the job – which involved "lifting and packing up boxes of alcohol and putting them through the online system" for eight hours a day – as "absolutely backbreaking" (Natasha, service-user, Dublin, 50s). This was as Ireland was emerging from a national lockdown and Natasha had been holding out for a receptionist job in a nearby gym that was due to shortly re-open. A friend working at the gym had assured her of getting the job once it reopened, but Natasha worried that her payments would be cut if she waited any longer:

'They were hounding and hounding … I thought, "I'm just going to have to get something because they are just going to send me off anywhere" … And I felt very threatened … that I could get cut off the labour for nine weeks if I refused to go for jobs that they were suggesting to me. So, I felt under so much pressure to literally take anything that would get them off my back until this sports centre one came up.' (Natasha, service-user, 50s, Dublin)

The experiences of Aisling and Natasha jar with assessments that the use of sanctions 'is very modest' (Cousins, 2019: 39) in Ireland. Insofar as neither Aisling nor Natasha were actually penalty rated, their experiences also convey how the potency of sanctions as devices of conduct conditionality stems not from their enforcement but their *possibility* 'as a coercive threat hanging over all jobseekers' (Finn, 2021: 77). That is, it is not primarily their application but their existence 'as a threat to prevent non-compliance' (Boland and Griffin, 2018: 100) which gives welfare conditionality its governmental power.

If workfare constitutes a means of 'administrative re-commodification' (Holden, 2003: 314), quasi-marketisation involves what could be considered the 'hyper-commodification' (McGann, 2021: 29) of claimants. This arises from its role in multiplying how claimants' labour is commodified by the state, to create new possibilities for extracting even further profit from non-employed labour.

When employment services are competitively tendered and funded via Payment-by-Results, jobseekers are effectively organised into purchasing lots 'for which private agents bid to win a share of the services to support them, discipline them and make money from them' (O'Sullivan et al, 2021: 7). Successful bidders win the right to sell the unemployed for profit in the very real sense of earning outcome payments and service fees that are higher than the investments they make in promoting claimants to potential employers. In this way, marketisation extends how the labour of welfare recipients becomes 'an object of calculation and exchange' (Adkins, 2017: 300).

Employment services markets therefore do more than just streamline administrative re-commodification. They transform the 'commodity status' of surplus labour by constituting an intermediary space where third parties (contracted providers) can buy and sell that labour 'in a manner that any other commodity might be sold in "free" markets' (Grover, 2009: 501). Put simply, they multiply the dividend that can be extracted from claimants' labour.

Again, this was something that several interviewees seemed all too aware of. As one person who had spent two years on JobPath put it, "You are just a number to be dealt with for financial reward" (Jim, service-user, 40s, Dublin). For these participants, outcome payments were interpreted as "commission" that providers extracted from selling them into jobs – "a horrific commodification of other people's circumstances" (Kevin, service-user, 50s, Tipperary). There was a palpable fury in how several spoke of their awareness that they were essentially a commodity: "They just want to chase this fee that they are getting. I believe they get €3,000 for every person they get into [employment] … I just don't think they care about the person; they care about the money" (Ray, service-user, 30s, Offaly). "They actually get commission for everyone they get off the labour. I was furious when I heard that. Then it all made sense. It was like, she didn't actually give two shits about me, she really didn't. She just wanted to get me off Jobseekers" (Natasha, service-user, 50s, Dublin).

Of course, third parties profiting from the exchange of labour has been a feature of capitalism since the emergence of labour hire firms in the early 1900s (Grover, 2009). But in the case of labour hire firms, jobseekers do at least have exit options and a formal right of refusal. In employment services markets, by contrast, the possibility of incurring sanctions means that claimants have little option 'but to cooperate in their state-sponsored hyper-commodification' (McGann, 2021: 29). This distinction was succinctly expressed by one interviewee in her account of being referred to JobPath just months earlier. Reflecting that she wouldn't mind so much if "it was part of a government agency", Hannah described how her "heart sank" when "the letter came through the door … It shattered me, it truly shattered me. I don't know whether this is relevant or not, but I feel like I'm after being sold by the state to this … company. And I'm furious as hell about it, but there is nothing I can do" (Hannah, service-user, 50s, Cork).

Governing (knaves) at a distance

The second point of intersection between workfare and marketisation is their underlying theory of motivation. Each begins from the assumption that claimants and service workers are somewhat deviant agents who cannot be relied upon to work hard without the use of external incentives. From this perspective, unemployment and benefit receipt are primarily viewed as motivational problems to be treated with behavioural remedies that appeal to agents' 'purposive rationality' (Morris, 2020: 276) rather than structural issues requiring demand management. Importantly, this diagnosis applies both to the motivations of claimants but also to the service workers tasked with supporting them to find employment (Le Grand, 1997, 2010; Wright, 2012).

The 'pathological' (Stambe and Marston, 2022: 4) theory of unemployment underpinning workfare is well-documented. It has its origins in 'underclass' theories of 'dysfunctional poverty' (Mead, 2014: 95), which date back to at least the Victorian era. Such theories resurfaced with force during the early 1980s via the arguments of Conservative welfare reformers such as Charles Murray and Laurence Mead, who each denounced claiming benefits as a 'moral failing' (Boland and Griffin, 2021: 51). The two differed over the degree to which they believed welfare recipients genuinely aspired to work, although they each attributed the rising welfare caseloads observed in America at the time to the generosity of payments and the fact that claimants had 'too many other sources of income … to work reliably unless programmes require them to do so' (Mead, 1986: 13).

Murray notoriously positioned welfare as a lifestyle choice made by claimants acting in response 'to the reality of the world around them' (1984: 162) and the very low wages on offer at the bottom of the labour market. Essentially, he regarded claimants as 'rational skivers' (Gaffney and Millar, 2020) who deliberately chose welfare over work whereas Mead argued that claimants genuinely aspired to work but were 'enfeebled' (Boland and Griffin, 2021: 51) by dependency and a fatalist 'belief that their fate turns on forces outside of themselves' (Mead, 1986: 146). Either way, both saw the solution as requiring a paternalistic 'politics of conduct' (Mead, 2014: 97) enacted though '"people changing" programs' (Hasenfeld, 2010: 163) of reform. Case managers were to become 'the "engineers" of advanced liberalism' (McDonald and Marston, 2005: 381) in this new politics of conduct, tasked with rehabilitating the agency of claimants by ensuring they 'do not malinger on welfare and become "dependent"' (Stambe and Marston, 2022: 3).

This attribution of unemployment to the idleness and failings of claimants has yet to penetrate Irish policy discourse to the extent that it has other liberal welfare regimes (although see Gaffney and Millar, 2020; Power et al, 2022). However, it is circulating beneath the surface of activation discourses and hiding in plain sight in the *Pathways to Work* statements as well as in political pronouncements such as the assertion made by a Minister for Social Protection that people 'come into the (social protection) system straight after school as a lifestyle choice' (quoted in Power et al, 2022: 649). The first *Pathways to Work* strategy similarly redirected attention away from the structural causes of unemployment by prescribing a need 'to encourage [jobseekers] to be more active *in their efforts* to find work' and criticising Ireland's previous 'passive' approach for 'the development of a significant core of long-term unemployed' (Government of Ireland, 2012: 10 emphasis added). Again, the implication was that it was insufficient work-effort on the part of claimants which was partly to blame for Ireland's rising unemployment.

The service-users interviewed for this book recalled being continuously reminded of this responsibility to be more active in their job-search efforts through the "veiled threat" (Donal, service-user, 30s, Clare) written in bold on referral letters. For instance, one interviewee who had participated in three different rounds of JobPath reflected on the "psychologically injurious" assumptions that DSP communications conveyed about the agency of claimants:

'They have this sentence in big black letters on every letter … It gives you the impression that you're naturally inclined to be lazy and stupid. And I don't feel that I'm naturally inclined to be lazy and stupid. But I think if somebody kept telling me that, it might have an effect on my dignity … "You're lazy and you're stupid. And if we don't keep kicking you, you won't even get out of bed in the morning". That's the impression that you get. And it's the only section in bold type.' (Padraig, service-user, 40s, Tipperary)

Padraig's remarks highlight how workfare is 'steeped in' (Marston and McDonald, 2008: 267) a theory of claimants' agency that is deeply stigmatising. Conduct conditions are legitimated by positioning claimants as either rational skivers who are wilfully unemployed, or idle dependents who are listlessly unemployed.

Such a presumption of 'bad agency' (Wright, 2012: 310) also implicitly lies behind the governance turn towards marketisation, although in this case it is the presumed idleness of service workers that is discursively targeted. As Le Grand argues, core to the NPM reform paradigm is 'a particular view of human motivation' (1997: 150) that assumes public service workers are 'knaves' motivated by little more than their own self-serving interest as opposed to the 'competent and benevolent' (1997: 155) professionals that proponents of classical public administration positioned them as. This questioning of the motivation of public service workers stems from public choice theory in economics, which grew to prominence in the 1970s and early 1980s as an influential critique of bureaucracy and the public provision of services. This was a time of rising public expenditure. Public choice theory, which assumes that all agents – regardless of whether they are politicians, bureaucrats, or entrepreneurs – are driven by 'rational utility maximisation' (Talbot, 2010: 62) sought to explain this rise in expenditure partly as a function of bureaucrats' rent-seeking behaviours. Public choice theorists argued that bureaucratic organisational structures emboldened public servants to try to maximise their salaries and personal power, meaning they could never be trusted to deliver 'what they are supposed to nor to serve the community' (Torfing et al, 2020: 60). This was due to the weakness of bureaucratic accountability mechanisms and their associated vulnerability to principal–agent dilemmas.

Principal–agent problems arise when there is a misalignment between the interests of shareholders (principals) and the interests of the managers (agents) running enterprises on their behalf. In listed companies, principals want to maximise profitability to increase dividends whereas managers seek to increase their salaries without a corresponding increase in work intensity. So, the self-interest of managers conflicts with the interests of shareholders insofar as it diminishes the profitability of the company. Public sector organisations are argued to be especially vulnerable to principal–agent problems due to the scale of the information asymmetries that exist in large bureaucracies, the diffuse nature of the principal's interests in the context of public services, and the public's weak control over administrators. In enterprises, the interests of principals and their agents are aligned through performance and accountability instruments. These include contracts detailing agents' obligations to principals, systems for measuring the performance of agents against key indicators (revenue or share price growth), and financial incentives (performance bonuses) for agents to pursue goals set by the principals. NPM and market governance approaches apply much the same logic to resolving principal–agent problems in the public sector: introducing performance measurement and performance-related pay within bureaucracies and controlling delivery agents through auditing systems and 'the incentives inherent to competitive markets and performance management' (Torfing et al, 2020: 61). The theory is that 'if the right "incentive" structures between "principals" (the government) and "agents" (public service organisations and workers) can be put in place, and agents' performance against these incentives properly measured, substantial improvements can be made' (Talbot, 2010: 63). To this extent, quasi-market structures and their associated regimes of performance 'targetry'

(Talbot, 2010: 63) are an attempt to harness the self-interest 'of those working in the system to the public good' (Le Grand, 1997: 159).

The extent to which public choice theory has informed quasi-marketisation in Ireland is not entirely clear. On face value, the argument for quasi-marketisation was pragmatic rather than theory driven. It was about filling a void in the capacity of the system that could not be met through increased public provision due to the then freeze on public sector hiring. Positioning the creation of JobPath "as a creature of the last recession", a DSP official explained that "what was attractive at the time was the capacity to scale up and scale down" (Jeremy, DSP). Nonetheless, an examination of the Fine Gael/Labour Government's post-2011 reform agenda reveals that public choice theory ideas were also circulating in the background to propel the case for wider public sector reform.

In its 2011 programme for government, the Fine Gael/ Labour Government championed the need for public services 'to become more transparent, accountable and efficient' so that they serve 'the common good, not sectional interests' (Government of Ireland, 2011: 28). Decrying the 'persistent under-performance' of Ireland's public services, it set out to 'pin down accountability for results at every level of the public service ... with clear consequences for success and failure' (Government of Ireland, 2011: 28). Thus, it traded on the (public choice theory) idea that rising public expenditure during the pre-crisis years was linked to the inefficiency of the public sector, the unchecked pursuit of self-interest by public servants, and a deficit of accountability for performance.

These were themes taken up by one of the policy stakeholders interviewed for this book, an independent advisor active in consulting with the DSP during the early years of the *Pathways to Work* reforms. He reflected on the multiple considerations informing quasi-marketisation, one of which was the need to create "some sort of incentive to get people to enthusiastically encourage people to search for work, and get it" (Lance, independent advisor). To reiterate his point, he compared "the days of FÁS" when:

> '[N]obody was watching what you achieved in terms of getting people back to work or getting people into employment. So, there would always be the tendency for agencies or organisations or bodies that are not driven by some sort of competitive incentive system to revert back into a fairly comfortable work environment where nobody was looking at the bottom line – which is, how many people do you get back into the jobs.' (Lance, independent advisor)

Regardless of whether such an incentive paradigm logic was indeed the original impetus for reform, measuring service providers against the 'bottom line of results' has clearly become the DSP's favoured means of steering providers. To this extent, when asked about future commissioning models beyond JobPath, a DSP official maintained "it would be difficult to envisage that we wouldn't have an element of Payment-by-Results for that … I don't think that would be really considered". Echoing central ideas from Osborne and Gaebler's *Reinventing Government* that 'Accountability must shift from inputs, such as line items, to outcomes and results' (Osborne, 1993: 354), he was dismissive of the LES' 'costs–met' funding model and the transaction costs associated with it:

> 'What we should be measuring is their employment performance. But what we seem to be measuring, or spend a disproportionate amount measuring, is why do they have such high energy bills, or they need a lot of software this year. … It's in nobody's interest to be wasting time on things like that. But it's just the necessity of a costs–met model … [that] the Department needs to monitor expenditure in a fairly detailed way, which kind

of distracts from what the focus should be on, which is employment outcomes.' (Jeremy, DSP official)

We can see from this discussion how workfare and quasi-marketisation are essentially 'cut from the same neoliberal cloth' (Soss et al, 2013: 138). To solve unemployment, each 'look[s] "downstream"' (Wright, 2012: 312) at the recalcitrant agency of welfare and administrative subjects. If welfare caseloads continue to rise, then this is a problem to be remedied by recalibrating the incentives for claimants to increase their job-search intensity. And if activation programmes fail to achieve policy goals this is because their administrative design is not adequately calibrated to 'serve the self-interest of the people delivering that policy' (Le Grand, 2010: 60). Claimants are to be governed as reluctant jobseekers who 'need to be financially incentivised to sell their labour' and delivery agents as self-interested knaves 'who need to be financially incentivised to place people in paid work' (Shutes and Taylor, 2014: 214).

Note

[1] 'Triple' activation denotes the extension of activation 'beyond the unemployed individuals who are policy's official subjects, to the organisation which are policy's implementers, to the street-level staff who are policy's putative producers' (Brodkin, 2013b: 11). However, most uses of 'double activation' incorporate the activation of delivery organisations *and* frontline workers so the terms are synonymous.

FOUR

Workfare meets marketisation

The previous chapter conceptualised the framework of 'double activation' as offering far more than a descriptor of the historical congruence between the activation turn in social policy and the marketisation turn in welfare administration. Analytically, it is concerned with how the two tracks of welfare reform are not just conjoined but mutually constitutive. In other words, it focuses attention on the role of marketised implementation structures in not just accompanying but *accelerating* the policy turn towards workfarist activation. The Irish case offers a rare natural policy experiment for exploring this dynamic in detail because of the co-existence of two employment services programmes operating under the same activation policy settings yet commissioned through distinct governance modes. Drawing on survey and interview research with frontline staff delivering JobPath and LES and service-users participating in the programmes, this chapter explores how the two employment services differed in practice at the coalface of delivery.

Formally, both services operated under the same activation policy setting in terms of requirements to develop PPPs with jobseekers and to provide them with job-search assistance for a period of 12 months. Yet, as detailed in this chapter, the two services differed in significant ways as to how they implemented this activation case management model. This was especially in relation to how they adjusted the balance between the demanding and enabling elements of activation (see Chapter One): whether they prioritised a regulatory approach anchored in job-search conditionality and the enforcement of conduct conditions or focused predominantly instead on 'employability building' through facilitating opportunities for jobseekers to pursue education, training, and work experience. Not that the different orientations are incommensurable. As outlined in Chapter One, activation models frequently combine enabling and demanding elements. Nevertheless, the data reviewed in this chapter suggests that the frontline workers in the different sectors of Ireland's mixed economy exercised their administrative discretion in distinct, patterned ways that tipped the balance between the enabling and demanding elements *in decisive ways*.

The chapter proceeds by first examining how the two frontline workforces approached the demanding elements of activation. In particular, the discussion focuses on the extent to which the JobPath and LES frontline staff reported that they used sanctions and conditionality with clients, and the differences in the intensity of activation (frequency of appointments and extent of job-search monitoring) between the two programmes as reported by delivery staff but also service-users. The second half of the chapter then turns towards the more enabling elements of activation, to consider whether there is evidence that JobPath and LES differed fundamentally in relation to prioritising 'work-first' over human capital development. In both cases, the interview and survey data provide robust evidence that a distinctly more workfarist approach was being enacted by the frontline workers delivering JobPath compared with how activation was being enacted by those delivering LES. The reasons why this was the case are the focus of Chapter Five, which explores the different managerial and performance regimes in which the two frontline workforces were embedded and the very different sets of occupational identities and worldviews that anchored the delivery of welfare-to-work in the two programmes.

Demanding activation

Reflecting on the intersection between workfare policies and quasi-market implementation reforms, Bredgaard and Larsen suggest that the outsourcing of delivery to market actors may be motivated in part by a political belief that private agencies will be 'tougher' in their use of 'sanctions, demands, and other motivational initiatives' (2007: 294). In other words, private delivery agents are expected to be more *demanding* on jobseekers than case managers working in public sector organisations, and particularly if those case managers are trained in social work or other 'professional moral frameworks' (van Berkel, 2017: 26) that stand opposed to the enforcement of conduct conditions (Larsen, 2013; Caswell and Larsen, 2017). For instance, Larsen argues that Denmark's introduction of a quasi-market in the early 2000s was in part motivated by a suspicion that social workers in municipal job centres were 'protecting the unemployed' (2013: 111). The OECD's review of Ireland's pre-crisis activation policies alluded to similar suspicions about a reluctance to impose sanctions among case officers in FÁS (Grubb et al, 2009: 85–86).

The reasons why private providers might be drawn towards more demanding strategies are several. One is that commissioners often tightly specify contractors' role in monitoring their clients' compliance with conduct conditions. Contractors may thus fear being disciplined themselves by the government purchaser if they are found to be too lenient in monitoring jobseekers' compliance with mutual obligations. In other words, there is a trickle-down effect as the monitoring of providers by the purchaser spills over into the monitoring of frontline staff by agency managers, and down to the scrutiny of jobseekers by advisors. It's a dynamic van Berkel describes as 'triple activation' (2013), and which agency executives identified in terms of the "flow down" of contract terms to their staff. For instance, the JobPath staff interviewed for this book reported being mindful of "trying to stay compliant" (Anna, JobPath advisor). As one explained, "we're contracted to the Department to basically do *their* contract" (Joanna, JobPath employer liaison and ex-advisor, emphasis added). "Everything that is part of the contract is monitored" (Liam, JobPath advisor), explained another.

A second reason why market providers might be drawn towards enacting more demanding approaches with clients is that behavioural demands such as intensive job-search obligations are low-cost intervention models. They require few investments in training or non-vocational support and offer a way for providers to maximise their revenues if clients can be relatively quickly 'hassled' into work. These hard-edged approaches won't work in many cases – particularly for people with complex barriers beyond a lack of work. But they offer a first port of call as a way of 'shaking the trees' (Murphy et al, 2011: 4) to determine if people are unemployed due to low job-search intensity or other, more structural needs.

Demanding time

Insights about the relative 'demandingness' of activation are offered by a range of survey and interview questions that frontline JobPath and LES staff were asked. Some addressed issues of enforcement, and the degree to which advisors were encouraged to be meticulous arbiters of compliance. Others addressed issues of frequency and intensity, such as how often participants were expected to attend appointments and other activities. Indeed, as Kaufman argues, fundamentally 'behavioural conditionality is about attendance' (2020: 210). Whatever tasks advisors may set, these all depend on service-users first attending case management appointments.

The frequency and duration of these meetings can be highly varied, resulting in programmes making vary different demands on unemployed people's time – something that policy and programme logics all too frequently assume unemployed people have plenty of to spare (Marston and McDonald, 2008). Marston and McDonald's research on people's experiences of Australian employment services goes on to highlight the sense of 'time being wasted as a result of mutual obligation requirements' (2008: 260). This speaks to both the perceived futility of participation from the perspective of service-users, as well as the amount of time *consumed* by meeting mutual obligations.

When interviewing Irish frontline staff, it quickly became apparent that the temporal demandingness of activation varied markedly between JobPath and LES. The JobPath providers operated on a higher frequency of client engagement than the LES organisations. Typically, LES mediators reported meeting clients at least "once a month" (Catherine, LES Mediator). This was the minimum contractual requirement although, as one manager explained: "you could work with people and seem them more if they need it" (Laura, LES Manager). Whether mediators did so was ad hoc, and case-by-case. Some even admitted to seeing clients *less frequently* than required: "If it's a thing where they are working away, they are happy with their job seeking skills ... or they are on a course, then you might see them every two months" (Sarah, LES Mediator).

But in JobPath, frequent appointments were the norm. One provider had a baseline of "an official appointment once every three weeks" (Liam, JobPath Advisor) while the other scheduled appointments "every ten days to two weeks" (Lisa, JobPath Advisor). The rationale was "that momentum keeps them moving", the implicit assumption being that unemployed people risked failing into idleness if they were not seen frequently by advisors: "At least they're coming in, and you know 'God I have to go in there now. I better have something to tell her, I better be doing something' ... because it's very hard, once you break the habit, to get back into it" (Lisa, JobPath Advisor).

This disparity in appointment frequency between JobPath and the LES might be interpreted as evidence that jobseekers were being parked by LES organisations. This is assuming that less frequent appointments disadvantage jobseekers in some way. However, as Sainsbury emphasises, what matters is not the frequency of appointments per se but 'the *quality* of meetings' (2017: 60). For those already close to employment, or who experience appointments as offering little benefit, frequent meetings may be experienced as interventions that are 'more harmful than helpful' (Kaufman, 2020: 214). This was certainly a perspective shared by many of the service-users interviewed, who repeatedly described their appointments with JobPath advisors as little more than "a box-ticking exercise" (Jim, service-user, 40s, Dublin) and "a waste of everyone's time" (Hugh, service-user, 40s, Cavan):

> 'There was a feeling that "In you come, right, out you go because I've got somebody else to do" … We'd talk about one or two things but nothing to do with [work]. It'd be more chit chat … I got to the stage where I could come in and be out in 15 minutes.' (Leonard, service-user, 60s, Kildare)

Beyond the frequency of appointments, another notable difference between how JobPath and LES staff engaged with their clients was that LES mediators generally met with jobseekers in private offices. JobPath advisors, by contrast, worked in open-plan offices that blurred the boundaries between public and private. Appointments were held with only "a divider between you and the other person sitting the other side of the desk" (Sarah, service-user, 40s, Limerick).

Previous research by the Irish National Organisation of the Unemployed suggests unemployed people can often prefer this approach as 'less formal' (INOU, 2019: 19). However, other international studies highlight the potential for open meetings to be experienced as a process of 'social suffering' (Wright et al, 2020: 284) characterised by feelings of anger, despair, and humiliation from having to discuss intimate, personal details in public. To this extent, some of the service-users interviewed for this book expressed feeling a "real lack of respect" in an environment where "everybody is telling their business to the whole world" (Beatrice, service-user, 30s, Dublin).

> 'You'd have people who maybe have behavioural kind of [issues], who would be really struggling emotionally. Maybe they wouldn't have literacy skills and maybe getting distressed … When the drunk fella starts kicking off, there is nowhere to go. So, you know, if that's the environment, you're appearing in … it just reinforces any pre-existing conditions or notions that you have that you are on the absolute bottom of society.' (Aisling, service-user, 30s, Dublin)

At a minimum, JobPath advisors met with clients every two to three weeks although it was not uncommon for them to report that some clients "could have an appointment with them every week" (Liam, JobPath Advisor). For instance, one former advisor recounted how she "often brought them into the centre twice a week, you know, and give them the time, 'Look, you can apply for this job'" (Joanna, employer liaison and former advisor, JobPath). As implied in Joanna's comment, the weekly attendance required of some clients was not limited to formal appointments but could include a "job-search session" (Anna, JobPath Advisor) on computers, either individually or in groups. This was something no LES clients had experienced, nor was it an approach ever mentioned by mediators. But it was a strategy that JobPath providers appeared to use with some frequency despite service-users roundly criticising it as "a total waste" (Cormac, service-user, 40s, Limerick). The approach disregarded the fact that they were already applying for jobs in their own time, while service-users claimed that there were seldom any vacancies listed on the computers that they were not already aware of:

'[Y]ou might only spend 10 minutes job-seeking because there might be no jobs available or the jobs that were available might have already been applied for. But you still had to sit at the computer for 40 or 45 minutes at least, even if it meant you virtually doing nothing. Because if you left early, your personal advisor then got it in the neck from his manager.' (Cormac, service-user, 40s, Limerick)

'They started me going through a process of having to come into the office to sit at a PC and do research on, I don't know what really, because a lot of the time I was just playing on the PC … I knew what I should be doing, and I wanted a job. But they insisted, and again, the threat of "If you don't do this, your benefits could be in question".' (Frank, service-user, 50s, Clare)

Demanding compliance

Service-users' comments about having "to show up [to job-search sessions] or they'd take your money away" (Aisling, service-user, 30s, Dublin) speak to questions of enforcement, and the extent to which JobPath and LES staff were prepared – and threatened – to report breaches of conduct conditions. This issue was further explored through a range of survey questions about the role of frontline staff in enforcing mutual obligations and the extent to which they were encouraged to actively police compliance. These survey data provide important insights into the differences in orientation between JobPath and LES staff, although they should be interpreted cautiously. This is partly because penalty rates were suspended at the time of the survey due to COVID-19. So, the questions relied on asking respondents about their behaviours in 'typical (non-COVID) times'.

Taking survey data at face value is also problematic insofar as self-reported responses are not always reliable proxies for what people do. On issues of sanctioning perhaps more than anything else, respondents may give the answers they feel they *ought* to give rather than reporting their behaviours. Nonetheless, these limitations are of less concern for comparative analysis of the kind reported here since they apply equally to the responses of both LES and JobPath staff; and the *differences* between their responses can still be revealing. The main limitation, however, is that one JobPath provider did not allow its staff to be asked about sanctioning. The provider maintained that contractors did not actually penalty rate claimants; that was a matter for the DSP. All providers did was "let the department know [about non-attendance] and then it's up to department to sanction them" (Joanna, JobPath advisor). That may be so to the extent that contracted providers do not sanction clients directly. Nevertheless, their role in reporting people to the DSP remains highly salient. What might first appear as a quasi-automatic and purely transactional process is in fact often replete with moments of discretion that accumulate to circumvent or intensify the enforcement of conduct conditions.

Bearing these limitations in mind, the survey data reported in Tables 4.1 and 4.2 show notable differences in both the level of reporting between JobPath and LES staff, as well as in their *dispositions* towards reporting clients for breaching mutual commitments/obligations.

As Table 4.1 shows, of the JobPath staff who answered questions on sanctioning, the vast majority (61 per cent) indicated that they were encouraged *not to be lenient* 'in reporting clients for breaching mutual commitments'. This compared with less than 29 per cent of LES respondents, whereas a sizably higher proportion of LES staff (39 per cent) reported that they were encouraged *to be lenient*. These differences in responses were statistically significant, and they

Table 4.1: Enforcement of conduct conditions

Whether office encourages staff not to be lenient or to be lenient in reporting clients for breaching mutual commitments?	JobPath (n = 33)	LES (n = 111)
1. Not to be lenient	15.2%	5.4%
2.	15.2%	6.3%
3.	30.3%	17.1%
4.	30.3%	32.4%
5.	3.0%	18.0%
6.	6.1%	9.0%
7. To be lenient	0.0%	11.7%
p = 0.008 (Fisher's Exact Test)		
Estimated proportion of clients (% caseload) that respondents would report for breaching mutual commitments in a typical (pre-Covid) two-week period	**JobPath (n = 27)**	**LES (n = 99)**
• Mean	3.6%	1.4%
• Mann-Whitney *U*-Test = 547, Z=-4.8, *p* < 0.001		
To what extent are the decisions you make about your clients determined by STANDARD programme rules and regulations?	**JobPath (n = 76)**	**LES (n = 106)**
1. Very little	1.3%	12.1%
2.	5.3%	11.2%
3.	17.1%	16.8%
4.	15.8%	26.2%
5.	25.0%	16.8%
6.	18.4%	11.2%
7. A great deal	17.1%	5.6%
p = 0.003 (Fisher's Exact Test)		

Source: Adapted from McGann (2022b)

were also echoed in reservations that LES mediators expressed in interviews about using the "big stick" of penalty rates. While a couple described having "no problem ticking that box" and that they treated it as "an automatic process" (Karen, LES Mediator), most claimed that they "would try and be lenient" (Michelle, LES Mediator) wherever possible:

'The penalty rate stick, I hated it but I have used it … We were supposed to use the penalty rate if there was two DNAs [did not attends]. I would do everything to avoid that. I would phone them. I would haunt them in the hope that it would make a difference.' (Sarah, LES Mediator)

'So de facto I use discretion. But every so often I get emails [from Intreo] saying "Do you realise that you've got three clients who have two DNAs, and you haven't referred them for consideration for penalty rating?" Or to be really frank, sometimes I avoid filling in the DNA within the timescales that we're supposed to … There is a tiny bit of discretion. I know I push it as much as I can.' (Michael, LES Mediator)

As implied in Michael's comment, LES staff claimed that they would bend the rules to avoid reporting clients for potential sanctioning. In Michael's case, this extended to taking a deliberately minimalist approach to jobseekers' PPPs. He would detail only the bear minimum of tasks and avoid specifying any targets that clients might fall foul of:

'In an ideal world [the PPP] should be a great resource. But in a controlled world, where people may actually suffer penalties, it's potentially dangerous. So, what I generally tend to do is keep the PPP as minimalistic as possible. I use phraseology like "Client is going to explore training options, client is an experienced electrician and seeking work in this area".' (Michael, LES Mediator)

Other mediators similarly differentiated between official PPPs, which might become "just another way of catching someone" (Anita, LES Mediator), and "the genuine ones" (Karen, LES Mediator) that they developed informally with clients. As one manager elaborated about the "very scant notes" her staff would record on official PPPs: "I think there's a reluctance from maybe staff in terms of what they put up there on the BOMi system, because they're so conscious of the compliance" (Laura, LES Manager).

JobPath advisors also exhibited discomfort at times about reporting clients. However, they saw themselves as having little wriggle room and tended to view the reporting process as just "part of our compliance that we have to do" (Paula, JobPath Advisor). Any wriggle room was further closed off by the fact that their managers "monitor all that sort of stuff" (Liam, JobPath Advisor) in terms of clients attending appointments and non-engagements being reported: "We really don't like to do that. But if clients are not engaging ... we have to do it. So, they're watching that as well. They're watching how many non-engagements you have" (Saoirse, JobPath Advisor).

Embedded in these comments is a sense of supervised rule adherence. This was also reflected in how JobPath staff responded to questions about the extent to which their decision-making was determined by standard rules and regulations. As reported in Table 4.1, over 60 per cent of the JobPath survey respondents reported that the decisions they made about clients – such as whether to report them for non-attendance – were determined by standard rules and regulations. Indeed, 17 per cent claimed that standard rules and regulations determined the decisions they made about their clients to 'a great deal' of extent. This compared with just 6 per cent of LES respondents and only a third of LES staff overall claimed that their decisions about clients were determined by standard rules and regulations.

All this suggests that JobPath staff exercised their discretion in a more compliance-orientated way than LES staff. This is further reflected in the different responses that JobPath and LES staff gave about the proportions of clients they would report for breaching mutual commitments/obligations in a given fortnight. On average, JobPath staff estimated that they would report just under 3.6 per cent of their caseload for breaching mutual commitments in a typical fortnight. Among LES staff, this proportion was estimated at just over 1.4 per cent (although mediators saw clients less frequently meaning there were fewer occasions for clients to fall foul of conduct conditions).

In international terms, less than 3.6 per cent is a relatively low percentage in terms of the proportion of advisors' caseloads that might be reported for sanctioning. To put this figure into perspective, when UK Work Programme staff were asked an almost identical question in 2016, they estimated that, on average, they would report approximately 5.6 per cent of their clients in a given fortnight (Lewis et al, 2017). In Australia, frontline staff claimed to have reported over 15 per cent of their clients for potential sanctioning (Lewis et al, 2016). Perhaps jobseekers in Ireland are just more compliant, although a likelier explanation is the much broader range of circumstances under which jobseekers in Australia can be sanctioned.

Australia has one of the strictest sanctioning regimes in the OECD in terms of the number of circumstances under which claimants can be reported for sanctioning (Senate Committee, 2019: 102). Of the 11 different circumstances listed in Table 4.2, close to 80 per cent of the Australian employment services staff surveyed in 2016 reported that they would refer a jobseeker for potential sanctioning in every circumstance bar 'a jobseeker leaves a training course' (Lewis et al, 2016). Irish frontline staff, by comparison, are far less likely to report that they would refer clients for breaching conduct conditions – although there are notable differences between the responses of JobPath and LES staff.

The data suggest that the circumstances under which LES staff would consider reporting clients for non-compliance are predominantly limited to missing appointments and not

Table 4.2: Circumstances when frontline staff would typically report clients for breaching mutual commitments

When would you normally report a client/ jobseeker for breaching their mutual commitments (when a jobseeker …)	JobPath (n = 24)	LES (n = 65)	p (Fisher's)
• Is dismissed from a job or training programme	36%	13%	0.023
• Refuses to apply for a suitable job	66%	25%	0.073
• Refuses a suitable job offer	96%	26%	<0.001
• Fails to commence an employment support programme, work experience, activity, or training	63%	28%	0.003
• Leaves a training course	17%	17%	1.00
• Fails to contact our office	46%	51%	0.814
• Fails to attend a job interview	65%	13%	<0.001
• Voluntarily leaves a job	42%	8%	<0.001
• Doesn't turn up for an appointment at our office	42%	78%	0.002
• Fails/refuses to sign their Personal Progression Plan	4%	55%	<0.001
• Does any of these for a second time	92%	78%	0.226

signing PPPs. These are activities and administrative routines that mediators must diligently record on the DSP's BOMi information management system. Yet only a minority of LES staff indicate that they would report clients for not fulfilling job-search related conditionalities, such as refusing to apply for a suitable job, refusing a suitable job offer, or failing to addend a job interview. This is in sharp contrast to JobPath staff, who predominantly indicated that they would report clients for breaches of job-search conditionality such as if a jobseeker 'refuses to apply for a suitable job' (66 per cent), 'fails to attend a job interview' (65 per cent), or 'refuses a suitable job offer' (96 per cent).

In interviews, service-users recounted how threats of "we have to let Social Welfare know if you are not showing up or you're not doing this and that" (Ray, service-user, 20s, Offaly) were "part of the armoury" (Ken, service-user, 40s, Dublin) used by JobPath. Several recalled examples of advisors threatening to report them for declining low-paid, low-skilled jobs that they had been recommended. In one example, a single mother with 20 years of retail management experience recounted being pressured to apply for a job on the production line of a jellybean factory. The factory was over an hour away by public transport and Natasha recalled a phone call with the agency's employer liaison "to sell" her the job that her advisor had arranged:

> "'These are not your average garden jellybeans; these are gourmet jellybeans,' that's what he said … My thoughts were well if they are gourmet jellybeans, why am I working for minimum wage, 40-hours a week, sitting on a production line when I trained so hard to not be in those positions, to be able to get into a management role. So, I got a rude text message … that she [advisor] would have to contact Intreo and tell them that I am refusing to go to an interview.' (Natasha, service-user, 50s, Dublin)

Rachel, a former JobPath client who subsequently transferred to disability payments, relayed a similar experience of being "warned" after declining to apply for a call centre job:

> 'They were quite annoyed with me. I tried to explain that from what I knew of call centres … People don't call call-centres when they're happy, and you have to be polite, and everything is timed and monitored. Just thinking about it made me even more anxious. And then they sent me to a sort of weird group meeting … we were basically told that we weren't doing well enough, and we weren't looking hard enough. This was a warning.' (Rachel, service-user, 30s, Tipperary)

Enabling activation

The forgoing discussion points to clear differences in the extent to which people participating in JobPath and LES experienced varying demands on their time, and in the application of conduct conditions and threats of sanctions for declining recommended jobs. However, it is not the use of demanding measures that differentiates the workfarist model from human capital approaches so much as the prioritisation of 'job-search intensity' (Raffass, 2016: 427) and rapid labour market attachment as the path to reintegration. Workfare models will include some enabling measures to support claimants in their search for work. Examples include job-search advice and basic training to gain the entry-level certificates – for instance in forklift driving, manual handing – needed to work in low-skilled occupations. Conversely, human capital approaches place the emphasis on building 'long-term employability' (Lindsay et al, 2007: 542) through more substantive forms of 'vocational skill formation' (Raffass, 2017: 350). The choice of approach, as Lødemel and Gubrium argue, 'reflects different understandings of the causes of worklessness' with workfare approaches being predicated upon assumptions of insufficient job-search effort whereas human capital approaches concern themselves with 'the effects of social exclusion' (2014: 329).

Work-first versus human capital development

The survey questions included a range of items designed to tease out whether frontline staff prioritised 'work-first' over human capital development, or vice versa. One such measure was a question asking respondents to evaluate which was the more important goal of their agency, on a scale from '1. To help clients get jobs as quickly as possible' to '7. To raise the education or skill levels of clients so that they can get the job they want in the future'. A second measure presented respondents with this scenario: 'After a short time attending your service, an average jobseeker is offered a low-skill, low-paying job that would make them better off financially'. Respondents were asked what advice they would give in this situation, again on a scale from '1. Take the job and leave welfare' to '7. Stay on benefits and wait for a better a better opportunity'. As Table 4.3 shows, JobPath staff responded to these questions in a way that suggested they were significantly more 'work-first' orientated than LES staff. This was despite almost all advisors maintaining in interviews that they focused on supporting "the customer to make a choice on their job" (Maria, JobPath Manager) and that they "don't want somebody to start a job if it's not the job for them" (Saoirse, JobPath Advisor).

This apparent emphasis on client choice was challenged by service-users, who frequently complained that their experience was of a programme where "their main goal is just beat you into any type of a job" (Ray, service-user, 20s, Offaly). With few exceptions, a great source of frustration to the service-users interviewed for this book was that "the employment on offer was kind of at the very bottom rung of the ladder" (Jim service-user, 40s, Dublin) and that there was "nothing about job satisfaction or the right job for you" (Claire, service-user, 50s, Dublin). To illustrate the point, a service-user in her 60s who had worked in community services gave the example of being told about "a farm down the road that was looking for mushroom pickers and that I should go and apply there" (Angela, service-user, 60s, Sligo). This was just one of the many examples that service-users gave of being directed towards low-skilled manual work or entry-level service jobs that they had no interest or experience in doing:

'I said, "Look, my college background is I studied mechanical engineering … At the same time, I kind of regret not getting into maybe counselling or youth work. Is there anything out there, a backdoor way to get into youth work?" And then she [advisor] comes along again with hotel receptionist, office administrator, deli

assistants ... nightshifts at an Applegreen petrol station.'
(Ray, service-user, 20s, Offaly)

'It was, "You know how to wash pots, go wash more
pots." And every time I said, "Well yes, I also speak a
couple languages and I would like to not solely focus on
washing pots", no.' (Aisling, service-user, 30s, Dublin)

The survey data reported in Table 4.3 lend credence to
these criticisms. When asked whether they would advise
jobseekers to take a low-skill, low-paying job or wait for a
better opportunity, the vast majority (72 per cent) of JobPath
respondents answered that they would encourage jobseekers
to take the low-skilled, low-paid job. Indeed, 44 per cent
indicated that they would do so in the strongest possible terms.
LES staff were more divided in their views. A slim majority (53
per cent) reported that they would lean towards recommending
jobseekers to take the job. However, 20 per cent reported that
they would advise jobseekers to remain on benefits while a
further 26 per cent were neutral between recommending
clients to take the job or remain on welfare.

In terms of which was the more important goal of their
agency – to help clients to get jobs quickly or to raise the
education or skill levels of jobseekers so that they can get the
job they want – the differences in response between LES and
JobPath staff were even more revealing. Among LES staff,
66 per cent reported that raising jobseekers' education or
skill levels was the more important goal of their agency. This
compared with just over 40 per cent of JobPath staff. Indeed,
just 14 per cent of LES staff indicated that their agency's priority
was to get clients into jobs as quickly as possible whereas 30
per cent of JobPath respondents reported this view.

It must be noted that, in comparison to quasi-markets in other
liberal welfare states, the survey data suggest that the work-first
orientation of JobPath staff is relatively muted. For instance,
when asked the same question in a 2016 survey, 52 per cent of

Table 4.3: Work-first versus human capital development orientation of frontline staff

Based on the practices in your office today, what would you say is the more important goal of your agency.	JobPath (n = 77)	LES (n = 112)
1. To get clients jobs as quickly as possible	3.9%	5.4%
2.	11.7%	1.8%
3.	14.3%	6.3%
4.	29.9%	20.5%
5.	15.6%	14.3%
6.	9.1%	24.1%
7. To raise jobseekers' education or skill levels so that they get the job they want in the future	15.6%	27.7%
Fisher's Exact Test $p < 0.001$		
After a short time attending your service, an average jobseeker is offered a low-skill, low-paying job that would make them better off financially. If you were asked, what would your personal advice to this client be?	**JobPath (n = 77)**	**LES (n = 111)**
1. Take the job and leave welfare	44.2%	24.3%
2.	18.2%	13.5%
3.	9.1%	15.3%
4.	19.5%	26.1%
5.	6.5%	10.8%
6.	2.6%	3.6%
7. Stay on benefits and wait for a better opportunity	0.0%	6.3%
Fisher's Exact Test $p = 0.023$		
In an average week, what proportion (%) of your time do you spend on working with other service providers (such as addiction, housing, or other community services)?	**JobPath (n = 69)**	**LES (n = 92)**
Mean	6.3%	12.9%

Table 4.3: Work-first versus human capital development orientation of frontline staff (continued)

In an average week, what proportion (%) of your time do you spend on working with other service providers (such as addiction, housing, or other community services)?	JobPath (n = 69)	LES (n = 92)
Mann-Whitney U-Test = 4312, Z = 4.02, p < 0.001		

Source: Adapted from McGann (2022b)

Australian employment services staff reported that getting clients into jobs as quickly as possible was more of a priority for their agency than supporting jobseekers to raise their education or skill levels. A staggering 92 per cent reported that they would encourage jobseekers to take offers of low-paid, low-skilled jobs rather than remain on benefits (Lewis et al, 2016). Likewise, among UK employment services staff, over 50 per cent reported that their agency prioritised rapid labour market attachment while 85 per cent reported that they would recommend jobseekers to take a low-skill, low-paid job (Lewis et al, 2017).

The Irish, UK, and Australian survey data are not directly comparable. The surveys were conducted at different points in time. So, too much should not be made of the differences in orientation between the three countries other than to acknowledge that Ireland's quasi-market is not especially 'work-first' by the standards of liberal welfare regimes. Nevertheless, in the national context of Ireland's mixed economy of activation, it does mark a significant embrace of 'work-first' and departure from a more historical focus on human capital development. This is further evidenced by the differences in how JobPath and LES staff responded to questions about working with other service providers.

Rice et al argue that 'the availability of flanking social services' (2017: 471) is a key ingredient in the capacity for service individualisation, which frequently requires other social services to be offered 'on top of employment services' (2017: 476). Of course, the availability of flanking social services is often outside the control of employment services. It frequently depends on external organisational capacity and the availability of other sources of government funding in local areas. Nonetheless, the extent to which different service providers are interacting with external social services still offers insights into the degree to which they are narrowly focused on labour market attachment or working in a more holistic way. Providers oriented by a 'work–first' approach would be expected to give negligible attention to addressing jobseekers' non-vocational barriers, and to therefore invest minimal time working with flanking social services. This indeed appears to be the case in relation to JobPath staff who, on average, estimated that they only spend 6 per cent of their time each week 'working with other service providers' such as addiction, housing, or other community services. This was less than half the proportion of time that LES staff reported spending each week working with other service providers (13 per cent).

Work experience, training, and education

The evidence to suggest that JobPath providers were enacting a distinctly more workfarist model of activation than LES providers was not limited to the survey data on whether frontline workers prioritised 'work–first' rather than human capital development. It also came from service-users' accounts of the qualitative differences in support they received from the two different employment services programmes. In particular, six of the service-users interviewed for this book had experience of both programmes. Among this group, a frequent observation was that compared with their experience of JobPath, the LES made them feel "that education is as good as job seeking" (Aisling, service-user, 30s, Dublin). Several had completed JobPath multiple times. One example was Shay, an LES client who had previously participated in three rounds of JobPath. Throughout his multiple periods on JobPath, Shay claimed to have never been offered any training other than a generic interview skills workshop and a referral to a manual handling course that he had already done. This contrasted with his experience of LES, where "they're not just restricted to the jobs" and he was being given "more options to look at" in terms of further training and work experience through "the Community Employment side of things" (Shay, service-user, 20s, Waterford).

Jim, another person with experience of both programmes, likened JobPath to "your strict father where the LES would be like your uncle minding you and getting you the stuff that he wouldn't normally get for you" (service-user, 40s, Dublin). One example of this was a local charity that Jim wanted to volunteer with, which he felt "wasn't a starter with JobPath but it is something that could be looked at with the LES in the form of a CE scheme" (Jim, service-user, 40s, Dublin). Jim was also being assisted to explore opportunities to return to education and to pursue a university degree, which was something that three of the ten LES service-users claimed to have been assisted with. Another example was Leonard, who was pursuing a social sciences degree. For Leonard, the path towards returning to education began with a year-long course in community development that was recommended to him by his mediator shortly after completing a life-coaching course that she had also referred him to. That coaching course had prompted him to consider retraining in community development, which Leonard's mediator subsequently helped him to pursue: "She rang me one day and said, 'Look, there's a year-long study course ... they only take 15 people, it's a full-time course' ... So, she got me the interview ... and I got one of the of the places" (Leonard, service-user, 60s, Dublin).

In other cases, people were supported to find work experience placements through either the TÚS scheme (short-term community work placements) or CE programme (community work placements of between one and three years). One example was Beatrice, a former JobPath client who wanted to pursue accountancy work. She had independently taken bookkeeping and payroll courses but lacked the work experience she felt she needed to secure an accountancy job. She raised this with her JobPath advisor but "it didn't go very far" whereas she was encouraged by her LES mediator to consider the CE programme as a way "to gain experience" (Beatrice, service-user, 30s, Dublin). Beatrice subsequently spent two-and-a-half years on the CE programme, working as a bookkeeper for a community organisation before progressing to a full-time accountancy job: "I wanted to study more, and the CE scheme is perfect for that because they push you to study ... I completed my certificate in accounting ... I completed the train-the-trainer, level 6, to train people. I've done the ECDL [European Computer Driving Licence]" (Beatrice, 30s, service-user, Dublin).

One reason why LES mediators may have been so keen to direct clients towards work experience placements is that the CE and TÚS schemes are frequently administered by local development companies on behalf of the DSP. As such, LES and work experience programmes are essentially managed by the same organisation. This co-management reinforces awareness of the CE and TÚS schemes among LES staff who, in interviews, elaborated on how they would "work very, very closely" (Siobhan, LES Mediator) with the CE and TÚS schemes as "their main kind of progression options" (Angela, LES Mediator) for people without recent employment experience: "Some of the older clients, it's hard enough because they may have been out of work five, ten years. Again, we're very lucky. We have the TÚS program. The TÚS supervisors are employed through the local development company. We can self-refer. I've seen that being a real plus for clients" (Michelle, LES Mediator).

In contrast to LES clients, few of the service-users interviewed for this book had been directed towards work experience, education, or training programmes while participating in JobPath – other than job-search skills workshops or low-level training in forklift driving or certificates in occupational health and safety "to get you into introductory things" (Rosemary, service-user, 30s, Louth) and "you had a job that was lined up, and you needed something like your safe pass" (Rachel, service-user, 30s, Tipperary). This limited support for upskilling was again a frequent source of frustration to service-users:

'That was the only thing that I was ever told to go to, was a CV one-day course ... I asked them was there any training courses, night-time training courses or part time training courses, that I could go on ... No, nothing.' (Siobhan, service-user, 50s, Laois)

'I was only in one workshop with them for the CV construction ... Other than that, I was never offered any kind of course, any kind of upskilling.' (Megan, service-user, 40s, Cavan)

As implied, the 'training' courses offered to JobPath participants were predominantly in-house workshops on job-search rather than vocational skills. This would be in the form of group sessions delivered onsite over several hours. At one office, these workshops were "running three to four times a week" (Joanna, employer liaison and ex-advisor, JobPath) while advisors from other offices likewise described an array of in-house workshops that clients could complete on "the job market, preparing them for work, CV building" (Anna, JobPath Advisor) or on "confidence, interview skills ... communication, and team-work skills" (Lisa, JobPath Advisor). These were routinely offered across offices and appeared to be a standardised formula offered to almost all clients. This was reflected by the fact that service-users who had been through multiple rounds of JobPath described repeating the same training on "CV writing, letter writing and interviews at the very start of both of the JobPaths" (Angela, service-user, 60s, Sligo) that they did: "Two years, the same thing. There's not really any difference like. It's just you do an interview course, how to apply for a job, a cover letter" (Sophie, service-user, 30s, Laois).

Some found aspects of this training helpful, although the workshops were predominantly experienced as "very, very, simple" (Hugh, service-user, 40s, Cavan) and at times deeply stigmatising in terms of the 'pejorative welfare tropes' (Redman and Fletcher, 2021: 14) that they conveyed about the agency of claimants:

'They had a big clock image like we were in playschool. You know, big hands at three, little hands at eleven, and she was going around the room and she was saying "Okay, what time do you get up?" Because obviously, the joke there is you're all unemployed so you're all getting up at midday to watch daytime telly … So, I said to her, "Well 6 am".' (Sarah, service-user, 40s, Limerick)

'The very first thing they said was "Now, you have to do your CV on a computer. You can't go doing a handwritten CV, that's not going to work." And I was like, "What the actual fuck am I at?" And then the second thing they said, "The other thing is, if you're going to do a CV it has to be on white paper. So, don't be submitting purple paper, or pink paper".' (Anna, service-user, 30s, Dublin)

These service-users' experiences of a heavily routinised and 'work-first' oriented programme echo the lived-experiences of activation reported by claimants in other Irish studies (for example Finn, 2021; Whelan, 2022). There is, of course, always a danger that qualitative studies of this kind will invariably be skewed towards documenting the most negative of service-users' experiences. This stems from the likelihood that it is people with an axe to grind who are the most willing to be interviewed about their experiences. Hence the importance of triangulating data from different sources, as this chapter has endeavoured to do.

Joining together the accounts of service-users with the survey responses and in-depth interviews with frontline workers paints a compelling picture of the very different ways that activation was put into practice by JobPath and LES organisations. The two employment services programmes may be formally anchored in the same active case management paradigm of 'intensive one-to-one support from an experienced employment services advisor' (Government of Ireland, 2012: 12). However, at the micro-level 'of everyday organisational life' (Brodkin, 2011: i253), those delivering the programmes strike the balance between the demanding and enabling elements of activation in very different ways. The network of LES appeared to retain the focus on training, education, and work experience that was a feature of Ireland's pre-crisis activation policies. Frontline workers in LES organisations also appeared more reluctant with their role as 'arbiters of claimants' compliance' (Kaufman, 2020: 212). The delivery model of JobPath, by contrast, appeared to exhibit a more rigid focus on enforcing conduct conditions and employing 'work-first' strategies underpinned by rapid labour market attachment and a heightened emphasis on training clients in how to job-search more intensively, and effectively.

In Chapter Five, the organisational factors contributing to these differences in how JobPath and LES staff interpreted activation policy on the ground are further unpacked. For, as Brodkin has long-argued, street-level workers 'do not do just what they want ... They do what they can' (1997: 24). Therefore, to fully appreciate how marketisation accelerates the turn towards workfarist activation we need to examine how quasi-market implementation structures reshape the agency and identities of frontline workers in ways that lead them to emphasise the more demanding elements of activation. It is to this issue that the book now turns.

FIVE

Remodelling agency at the street-level

The experiences of service-users and approaches of frontline staff discussed in Chapter Four showed that the model of employment support delivered under quasi-market conditions was distinctly more workfarist in orientation than the type of support that was provided by not-for-profit organisations in other parts of Ireland's mixed economy of activation. The JobPath model may not have been especially workfarist when measured against quasi-markets in other liberal welfare states. But it was nonetheless a significant departure from how the community organisations delivering LES were working with the long-term unemployed. So why did quasi-marketisation produce these policy effects? How did JobPath's procurement model – competitive tendering, price-bidding, and performance-based contracting – spill over into organisational practices to adjust the balance between the enabling and demanding elements of activation?

These are the core questions addressed in this chapter, which zooms out from the micro-level of caseworker-client interactions to consider issues of organisational dynamics and the recruitment practices and performance measurement regimes of JobPath and LES organisations. In so doing, the chapter draws on the Irish case to engage with wider debates about the disciplining effects of managerialism and performance measurement on frontline discretion (Dias and Maynard-Moody, 2007; Brodkin, 2011; Soss et al, 2013; Caswell and Høybye-Mortensen, 2015; van Berkel and Knies, 2016; O'Sullivan et al, 2019). It also offers a commentary on the ambiguous 'professional' status of activation work (van Berkel and van der Aa, 2012; Nothdurfter, 2016). In particular, the second part of the chapter focuses on how the procurement of employment services via price-bidding and competitive tendering fractures the kinds of occupational backgrounds and normative understandings that street-level workers bring to their work (Schram, 2012; Schram and Silverman, 2012; Greer et al, 2017; O'Sullivan et al, 2021). The upshot is what Noordegraaf terms 'controlled professionalism', as workers are managed not as professionals with recognised qualifications and skills but as 'employees with clear roles and responsibilities in turning organisational inputs – money, resources – into tangible results' (2015: 191).

The chapter develops the argument that both the disciplining effects of performance measurement *and* the fracturing effects of quasi-marketisation on the 'professional' identities of street-level workers are critical to understanding how marketisation reshapes agency at the street-level. It invokes the language of *agency* rather than the more conventionally-used term of 'discretion' (Maynard-Moody and Musheno, 2000; Evans, 2016) – in the sense of autonomy or decision-latitude – to emphasise that the concern is as much with a 'politics of professionalism' as it is with a 'politics of discretion'. Put simply, the choices that street-level workers make when putting policy into practice are shaped as much from below by their internal 'moral dispositions and working identities' (Kaufman, 2020: 212) as they are disciplined from above by systems of external accountability and performance measurement. This is not to say that the disciplining effects of performance measurement are inconsequential, far from it. Simply that performance measurement is only *part*, albeit a key part, of the story of how market governance reshapes agency in policy delivery.

Performance measurement and the politics of discretion

Research on the intersection between the two tracks of welfare reform frequently focuses on how 'the disciplinary turn of the global workfare project has been achieved, in part, through the disciplining of street-level workers' (Kaufman, 2020: 208). Key to this disciplining of street-level workers has been the rise of managerial surveillance and deployment of increasingly tighter forms of performance measurement to steer frontline behaviour (Dias and Maynard-Moody, 2007; Soss et al, 2013; Fuertes and Lindsay, 2016; Greer et al, 2017). Although performance measurement is often associated with the measurement of actors against specified targets reflecting organisational goals, there are several different dimensions to performance measurement. Lewis argues that performance measurement should be understood as a social structure involving a cascading 'chain' (2015: 9). The apex of this chain is the setting of policy and strategy by governments and organisations, and the decisions they make about what to value, the indicators that will be used to measure it, and the 'system rules that attempt to measure what is valued' (Lewis, 2015: 9). All these are then signalled to the 'the measured' who respond to measurement criteria and targets based on the understandings they develop from a variety of sources of the social structure of performance measurement in which they are embedded.

Approached as social structures in this way, performance measurement systems involve far more than systems for quantifying the processes, outputs, or outcomes produced by individuals or organisations. Among other things, they comprise the information management systems used to record data; the indicators by which people and organisations are measured (and whether their purpose is to determine payments, benchmark performance, or merely convey information);

the rewards and punishments (financial, reputational) that are contingent on measured performance; and the performative role of performance measurement within organisational cultures. The intensity of performance measurement systems is therefore a function of not just the number of metrics or the scale of targets that are set. It also depends on the administrative burdens and transaction costs associated with recording performance data as well as the degree of financial, managerial, reputational, or social pressure on the 'measured' to perform.

In quasi-markets, the 'chain of performance measurement' (Lewis, 2015: 9) extends all the way from the government purchaser to the organisations that are contracted, to the staff working at the frontline. This is insofar as organisations which are held accountable for adhering to minimum servicing standards or which are paid by outcomes 'will in one way or another send signals to workers about the performance expected form them' (van Berkel and Knies, 2016: 63). In this way, the use of market governance instruments to steer delivery organisations funnels into the use of corporate governance instruments (targets, management by objectives) by organisations to internally direct their staff.

'Supervised' discretion

A core question about performance measurement concerns how it *alters* what people do. Critics argue that street-level workers have become so subject to 'direction and surveillance from managers, that discretion has all but disappeared' (Evans, 2016: 281). This is a little too fatalistic. The concern is not so much that street-level workers no longer have any autonomy but that the measurement of their performance has become so ubiquitous that they make *different* decisions in light of their awareness 'of being observed and evaluated' (Soss et al, 2011b: i226). In other words, performance measurement reshapes frontline decision-making not through overriding but manipulating discretion. An illustration of this 'reactive conformance' (Asselineau et al, 2022: 10) was provided by one advisor, who described the pressures staff were under to set tasks for jobseekers each meeting just so that advisors were *seen to be* progressing clients:

> 'Part of our job, is to every time you meet the client, set a new task. And it can be as small as add something new to a CV … But because you're expected to do a task every time you speak to someone, you can be kind of just giving them a silly task for the sake of it.' (Carl, JobPath Advisor)

The 'tasks' were the activities in clients' PPPs, which were recorded on tabs in providers' information management systems. Organisational managers could view these client files and run reports on advisors' caseloads, which they regularly did:

> 'I would do checks on people's customers. Their journeys, what they're doing, what interventions have been put in place, what information, advice and guidance has been offered.' (Trish, JobPath Manager)

> 'There are structures in place, and we have to do x amount of; whether it be your tasks, put in the goals … Your centre manager ultimately at the end of the day is watching us.' (Saoirse, JobPath Advisor)

In these examples, it was frontline workers' adherence to work process standards rather than their achievement of outcomes that was being monitored. The focus was on activities and holding workers procedurally accountable for complying with minimum servicing standards. In terms of clients' PPPs, advisors were expected to routinely "be sticking in a task of some sort" (Carl, JobPath Advisor) as "evidence that you're helping the customer to progress" (Trish, JobPath Manager). This administrative record could then be used as proof to the government purchaser that "here's their progression plan, here's what they've done" (Maria, JobPath Manager); that clients had not been left idle. However, the extent to which this was monitored resulted in advisors setting tasks they openly admitted were futile, as the activity monitoring of staff cascaded into the activation of claimants. As Carl explained: "Every three weeks or so, you should be sticking in a task ... That stuff is fine to do when you are giving them worthwhile stuff to do. But some of the stuff you're just creating for the sake of putting in a task" (Carl, JobPath Advisor).

"I don't think its progression at all; it's the illusion of progression", admitted Carl. It was a sentiment echoed by several LES mediators, who were similarly frustrated by the extent to which they were obligated to record data on information management systems so that work processes could be audited and verified. This shifted the emphasis of meetings away from the provision of employment guidance towards the documentation of administrative conformance:

> 'The whole administration of seeing people and recording stuff on BOMi [information management system] ... making sure it's updated with information; I'm finding that all of this is detracting then from "What are we doing to get people off the dole?" ... It's like feed the Tamagotchi and forget about the core reason of why we are there.' (Karen, LES Mediator)

Despite the parallels in the activity monitoring of JobPath and LES staff, the survey data did point to significant differences in the *intensity* of oversight they were subject to. JobPath managers appeared to pay closer attention to what their staff were doing on a more regular basis, with 66 per cent of JobPath staff surveyed reporting that they strongly agreed that their 'supervisor knows a lot about the work I do day-to-day' (see Table 5.1). This compared with just 30 per cent of LES respondents and the responses of JobPath staff also indicated that they were more likely to defer to their supervisors when

Table 5.1: Supervisory oversight of frontline staff

The lines of authority are *not* clear in my work	JobPath (n = 77)	LES (n = 111)
• Strongly agree	2.6%	11.7%
• Agree	5.2%	9.0%
• Neither	2.6%	14.4%
• Disagree	33.8%	40.5%
• Strongly disagree	55.8%	24.3%
$p < 0.001$ (Fisher's Exact Test)		
My supervisor knows a lot about the work I do day-to-day	**JobPath (n = 77)**	**LES (n = 110)**
• Strongly agree	66.2%	30.0%
• Agree	19.5%	44.5%
• Neither	2.6%	10.0%
• Disagree	5.2%	9.1%
• Strongly disagree	6.5%	6.4%
$p < 0.001$ (Fisher's Exact Test)		
When I come across something not covered by the procedural guide, I refer it to my supervisor	**JobPath (n = 77)**	**LES (n = 110)**
• Strongly agree	55.8%	26.4%
• Agree	42.9%	52.7%
• Neither	0.0%	13.6%
• Disagree	0.0%	6.4%
• Strongly disagree	1.3%	0.9%
$p < 0.001$ (Fisher's Exact Test)		

Source: Adapted from McGann (2022a)

unsure of what to do. When asked if they referred issues not covered by procedural guidelines to their supervisor, 56 per cent of JobPath staff strongly agreed that they did. This compared with just 26 per cent of LES staff, who were more ambivalent about the extent of hierarchical supervision in their workplaces. Indeed, one in five (21 per cent) agreed or strongly agreed that the lines of authority *were not clear* in their workplace whereas almost 90 per cent of JobPath staff disagreed or strongly disagreed with the view that the lines of authority were unclear in their work. These differences in responses were all statistically significant, indicating that JobPath staff perceived that they worked under greater managerial scrutiny than their LES counterparts.

Targets and outcomes measurement

Turning from activity monitoring to outcomes and targets, the hope is that performance measurement will motivate people to work in more productive ways. As Behn argues, the real 'reason that managers set performance targets is to motivate, and thus to improve' (2003: 588). Yet performance measurement does not just result in the same things being done more efficiently or more effectively; workers also start 'to do different things' (van Berkel and Knies, 2016: 64). This arises from how 'the pressures of competition, the prospects of incurring rewards or penalties, the awareness that one is being closely monitored' (Soss et al, 2013: 126) can all work to reshape what Brodkin term's the 'calculus of street-level choice' (2011: i259). Recognising this brings into view the political effects of performance measurement, and its potential to bring about far-reaching changes in the distribution of benefits, resources, and sanctions that street-level workers enact on the ground.

In the case of welfare-to-work, a core concern is the preoccupation with job placement and off-benefits metrics as the key indicators of performance. For instance, Soss, Fording, and Schram's body of research on the intersection between performance measurement and sanctioning in the US state of Florida points to a correlation between the intensification of performance measurement and the sanctioning of welfare-to-work clients. This is both over time across the state, and between organisations subject to different degrees of performance pressure (Soss et al, 2011a, 2011b, 2013). Following the introduction of a more performance-driven welfare-to-work programme during the early 2000s (in terms of placement targets and payments tied to outcomes), they found a rise in sanctioning at the state level. Moreover, programme participants were more likely to be sanctioned if they were clients of for-profit providers rather than not-for-profit organisations Yet, when interviewed, very few of the case managers that Soss and colleagues spoke with expressed any belief in the efficacy of sanctions. Rather, their accounts of why they used sanctions suggested that they turned to sanctions as a 'last resort' and in the face of performance pressures. With little formal training and few resources to address their clients' problems, case managers turned 'to the most basic threat' they could wield and out of frustration that they were 'being held accountable while the client is not' (Soss et al, 2011b: i224).

In a British context, Redman and Fletcher have shown how a shift towards measuring the performance of Jobcentre Plus offices based on 'off-benefit flows' partly contributed to a rise in sanctioning rates within local offices. This was insofar as it was simpler for advisors to meet targets by 'finding ways to sanction claimants and/or dissuade claims' (Redman and Fletcher, 2021: 13), rather than focusing on moving people off benefits through supporting them into work.

Beyond sanctions, performance measurement systems may induce street-level workers to prioritise workfarist approaches through their so-called 'tunnel vision' effects: when actors respond to targets by zoning in on those aspects of their work that are measured at the expense of other valuable, but unmeasured, aspects of their job. The problem here for attempts to steer discretion through targets and performance measurement is the difficulty of specifying which aspects of frontline work matter, and capturing those in quantitative measures (Brodkin, 2008). If job placements or appointment attendance are primarily what is counted, street-level workers may focus their energies on ensuring clients fulfil appointments and search for whatever (low-paid) jobs are available. Meanwhile, interventions which might narrow people's distance from employment without guaranteeing a job, such as referrals to flanking social services, may become neglected; especially if there is uncertainty over whether actions will deliver tangible outcomes within the reporting timeframes of contracts.

The upshot is what Dias and Maynard-Moody term a 'performance paradox' (2007: 189). Behaviour is redirected towards the achievement of short-term outcomes 'at the expense of longer-term' (Talbot, 2010: 191) policy goals. The most well-documented performance paradox in the context of welfare-to-work delivery is the issue of providers and frontline staff adapting to performance measurement by 'creaming' their most job ready clients and 'parking' those they perceive as being more difficult cases. Jobseekers thus end up being targeted 'in inverse proportion to need' (Greer et al, 2018: 1429) with the result that public resources are withheld from the very cohorts that governments most want to activate into employment.

'Unseen' work

The myopic, tunnel vision effects of performance measurement are captured by the adage *what gets measured gets treasured*. The problem is that 'not everything that counts can be counted' (Asselineau et al, 2022: 7). So, critical dimensions of performance go 'unseen' (Brodkin, 2008: 323), as the frontline staff interviewed for this book frequently observed.

Among LES staff especially, there was widespread criticism that the targets specified in their contracts were "horrendous" (Trevor, LES Coordinator) and "pure nonsense" (Michael, LES Mediator). This was not in the sense that they paid little heed to them. To the contrary, they repeatedly reported that "chasing the job numbers is part of the job" (Siobhan, LES Mediator).

Otherwise, if "targets were down ... we're in trouble with our contract basically" (Fiona, LES Manager). LES staff claimed to be all too frequently reminded of this since the DSP took over responsibility for employment services contracting following the demise of FÁS. One manager described the DSP as coming "in like a big boot" (Laura, LES Manager) in terms of its approach to contract management. A mediator from another LES organisation reflected on the parallels between the use of sanctions to activate jobseekers and the threats of contract withdrawal faced by employment services providers:

'You hear in the ether about LES that are failing to reach targets, and they've been reduced to six-month contracts. So, it's a sense of fear. What I actually find ironic is that the same fear that the *Pathways to Work* process has generated within clients is also getting more and more replicated within the organisations that are supposed to be servicing those clients.' (Michael, LES Mediator)

Besides the pressures to meet targets, LES staffs' main criticism was that the target they were set seemed to have been "pulled out of the air" (Eileen, LES Coordinator). It was a uniform target by which the performance of all LES was measured – of placing at least 30 per cent of their caseload into full-time employment of indefinite duration. The target took no account of discrepancies in the profile of clients on different office's caseloads, nor was there any recognition of structural differences in the various labour market contexts that the different LES operated in. Hence, from the perspective of frontline staff, whether targets were achieved was more a reflection of arbitrary differences in "the breakdown of the caseload rather than the service or the abilities of the individual" (Michael, LES Mediator). Employment services staff were also acutely aware that other significant dimensions of frontline work, such as supporting people to return to education or gain work experience as a step towards reintegration were "just completely undervalued" (Michelle, LES Mediator). Indeed, they were actively disincentivised:

> 'The target of full-time employment was set by the powers that be to get people off [payments] ... That's nothing to do with the stepping-stone of somebody going from unemployed with an addiction, to part-time work and stable, to maybe, if they kept that going, full-time work. That whole life process doesn't take people off the Live Register, so it doesn't get counted ... What we do is you keep an eye on the targets ... And when you are doing that then you have the space to look after the more vulnerable.' (Fiona, LES Manager)

Embedded in Fiona's comment is a view of targets as *thresholds* to be satisfied – "to keep officialdom off your back" (Fiona, LES Manager) – rather than exceeded. Indeed, there were few incentives for LES staff to focus on job placements once their 30 per cent target had been met, particularly given the well-known problem of the 'ratchet effect': where people try to avoid over-reaching their targets so as 'to avoid too high targets in the future' (Talbot, 2010: 191). Confidence in being able to meet their targets gave LES staff scope to explore other progression options that weren't officially measured. This was less possible for JobPath staff, whose targets were "not set in stone" but fluctuated monthly "according to what's going on out there in the employment marketplace" (Norelle, Employer Liaison, JobPath).

In comparison to LES staff, JobPath staff displayed a less critical orientation towards targets. This perhaps reflected the fact 'that few had any experience of delivering employment services prior to JobPath, or under conditions where their success in placing clients into jobs was not closely monitored' (McGann, 2022a: 83). They were, to an extent, habituated to targets with many of the advisors interviewed for this book having previously worked in sectors such as retail, sales, and telemarketing where targets were the norm:

'Obviously because I'm from a telemarketing background – it was all targets – I suit the job well.' (Joanna, JobPath Employer Liaison and ex-advisor)

'[M]aybe it's because I come from retail and I come from a target driven area, I do focus on trying to get the jobs in and trying to hit them targets. And I know there's other people that just don't really ... they just won't chase, chase, chase.' (Carl, JobPath Advisor)

One or two acknowledged feeling "very conflicted" about the fact that "when you whittle it down really, it comes down to ... the numbers of jobs that we get" (Saoirse, JobPath Advisor). There were "two sides to the business", as one advisor put it, that required carefully balancing their "duty of care to the clients and to the community" against the fact "that I have to reach my job targets" (Anna, JobPath Advisor). But, generally, JobPath staff accepted the logic of performance targets as a managerial tool that "keeps you on your toes, which is good" (Liam, JobPath Advisor). Moreover, the use of performance measurement in this way extended beyond tracking whether individual workers had achieved their personal targets. Managers would also seek to motivate staff by using performance targets as means to catalyse internal competition and "a friendly rivalry" (Carl, JobPath Advisor) between staff for peer group recognition.

Occasionally, staff's performance as "the one who got the most jobs in the last quarter" or month would be rewarded materially in the form of "voucher just to say thank you" (Anna, JobPath Advisor). However, the principal currency of recognition was the symbolic conferral of status through "accolades like employee of the month" (Norelle, JobPath Employer Liaison). As one manager elaborated:

'They are reasonably competitive. It's not about the office target I don't think. It's about beating [their co-workers] ...

That's where I would have the fun with them ... I would go "What time was your last appointment? [Name], that was a fantastic result you had today, or yesterday ...you better leave early." Then I'll go silent. Next thing you'll hear, "But I did [target]". "Did you so? I didn't notice that." ... So, we have a bit of banter about it, and they openly want to say what they achieved this week.' (Maria, JobPath Manager)

Commodified performance

The survey data reported in Table 5.2 point to further sources of difference between the performance measurement regimes that JobPath and LES staff worked under. One particular point of difference is the degree to which JobPath staff were cognisant of 'the commodity value of their performance' (McGann, 2022a: 85). This in the sense that they took note of actions with clients that would produce *payable* employment outcomes and reported that their employer paid attention to the financial returns that they personally generated for the organisation.

Both JobPath and LES staff reported that numerical targets influenced their work, with no significant differences in their responses. However, on questions addressing the financial implications of their performance for their employer, the differences in responses were far greater. For instance, when asked whether 'more and more the objective in this job is to maximise the organisation's financial outcomes', 21 per cent of JobPath respondents agreed or strongly agreed that this was the case. A small majority (52 per cent) rejected this view, although this proportion paled in comparison to the 72 per cent of LES staff who rejected the idea that 'more and more the objective in this job is to maximise the organisation's financial outcomes'.

Likewise, when asked whether they were aware that their organisation paid attention to the income they generated by placing clients, over 80 per cent JobPath respondents – but only 9 per cent of LES staff – agreed or strongly agreed that this was the case. The responses of JobPath staff also suggested that they

Table 5.2: Targets and performance measurement

In my job, I am NOT influenced by numerical targets	JobPath (n = 77)	LES (n = 111)
• Strongly agree	7.8%	10.8%
• Agree	22.1%	23.4%
• Neither	18.2%	25.2%
• Disagree	45.5%	32.4%
• Strongly disagree	6.5%	8.1%
p = 0.47 (Fisher's Exact Test)		
I do tend to take note of actions with clients that will generate a payable outcome/reach an employment outcome target for the office	JobPath (n = 77)	LES (n = 110)
• Strongly agree	11.8%	8.2%
• Agree	47.4%	24.5%
• Neither	26.3%	22.7%
• Disagree	10.5%	25.5%
• Strongly disagree	3.9%	19.1%
p < 0.001 (Fisher's Exact Test)		
I am aware that my organisation pays attention to the income I generate by placing clients	JobPath (n = 76)	LES (n = 110)
• Strongly agree	25.0%	3.6%
• Agree	55.3%	5.5%
• Neither	10.5%	26.4%
• Disagree	5.3%	23.6%
• Strongly disagree	3.9%	40.9%
p < 0.001 (Fisher's Exact Test)		
More and more the objective in this job is to maximise the organisation's financial outcomes	JobPath (n = 77)	LES (n = 111)
• Strongly agree	6.5%	1.8%
• Agree	14.3%	6.3%
• Neither	27.3%	19.8%
• Disagree	41.6%	36.9%

Table 5.2: Targets and performance measurement (continued)

More and more the objective in this job is to maximise the organisation's financial outcomes	JobPath (n = 77)	LES (n = 111)
• Strongly disagree	10.4%	35.1%
p < 0.001 (Fisher's Exact Test)		

Source: Adapted from McGann (2022a)

took such financial factors into greater consideration when determining what actions to take with clients. For instance, 59 per cent of JobPath respondents agreed or strongly agreed that they 'do tend to take note of actions with clients that will generate a payable outcome or reach an employment outcome target for the office'. This compared with just 33 per cent of LES respondents. Indeed, only 14 per cent of JobPath staff reported that they did *not* take note of actions with clients that would generate a payable outcome or reach an outcome target whereas 45 per cent of LES staff claimed not to pay attention to whether their actions would lead to an outcome payment or the satisfaction of a performance target.

For JobPath staff, the principal means of achieving targets and generating business revenue is through achieving job placements. So, one logical consequence of advisors' heightened awareness that frontline actions carried financial value – that was being monitored by their employer – could be a narrow service delivery focus on *rapid* job placements. Indeed, this was a concern often expressed by LES mediators and service-users about the outcomes-based payment model underpinning JobPath. Namely, that it resulted in advisors "looking for the quick fixes, get them into Tesco's because I have target" (Catherine, LES Mediator) or that, as one service-user put it, "You could come in with a PhD and be told that you have to go work in McDonald's" (Jim, service-user, 40s, Dublin).

To further explore this intersection between the commodification of advisors' performance and a 'work-first' orientation towards clients, a correlation analysis was run using Spearman's rank–order correlation to test for any associations between the items on frontline workers' internalisation of the commodity value of their performance, and the measures discussed in Chapter Four on whether frontline staff, and the agencies that they worked for, prioritised rapid job placement over helping jobseekers to gain the skills and qualifications needed to obtain their preferred job. As Table 5.3 shows,

Table 5.3: Associations between commodity value of performance and 'work-first' disposition

	Whether more important agency goal is to (1) help clients get jobs as quickly as possible or (7) raise jobseekers' education or skill levels to get the job they want in the future	Whether would advise clients to (1) take a low-skill, low-paying job or (7) stay on benefits and wait for better opportunity
Aware that organisation pays attention to income generated by placing clients (1. Strongly agree to 5. Strongly disagree)	rs = 0.32 $p < 0.001$	rs = 0.23 $p = 0.002$
Take note of actions with clients that will generate a payable outcome/reach a target (1. Strongly agree to 5. Strongly disagree)	rs = 0.26 $p < 0.001$	rs = 0.16 $p = 0.031$
Objective of job is increasingly to maximise the organisation's financial outcomes (1. Strongly agree to 5. Strongly disagree)	rs = 0.20 $p = 0.007$	rs = 0.13 $p = 0.093$

Note: Adapted from McGann (2022a)

there was a moderate but significant correlation between the degree to which respondents agreed that their organisation paid attention to the income they generated by placing clients and the two 'work-first' measures on whether the more important goal of their agency was to help clients get jobs as quickly as possible and if they would generally advise clients to take a low-skill, low-paying job rather than remain on benefits and wait for a better opportunity. Likewise, there was also a correlation between respondents' answers on these two 'work-first' measures and the extent to which they reported taking note of actions with clients that would generate a payable outcome or reach a target. The degree to which frontline staff reported that the objective of their job was increasingly to maximise financial outcomes for their organisations was also correlated with whether frontline staff perceived that the more important goal of their agency was to help clients get jobs as quickly as possible, although it was not significantly correlated with whether advisors would recommend clients to take a low-skill, low-paying job.

In short, the data suggests that it is not performance targets per se that orientates street-level workers towards workfarist strategies but the extent to which they are aware of their actions carrying financial worth for their employer. Seeing clients as commodities with exchange value corresponds with a workfarist disposition towards encouraging claimants to sell their labour to employers as quickly as possible.

The politics of professionalism

The preceding discussion has demonstrated that one critical way in which quasi-market implementation structures reshape the agency of frontline workers is through the new systems of performance measurement that they embed within delivery organisations. The increasing accountability of workers to targets and more intensive forms of managerial oversight and performance monitoring disciplines discretion by strategically manipulating decision-making towards the achievement of organisationally defined targets and ends. However, these are not the only ways in which governance reforms potentially remodel frontline agency and choice. Other important aspects include the effects of governance reforms on the composition of the frontline workforce and the growing use of 'standardisation tools' (Mik-Meyer, 2018: e283) such as assessment protocols and profiling instruments, the use of which has become near ubiquitous in the delivery of welfare-to-work. This has important implications for the extent to which frontline work essentially involves the performance of administrative routines rather than a 'professional' practice (Caswell et al, 2010; Høybye-Mortensen, 2015; Mik-Meyer, 2018), as the remainder of this chapter considers beginning with a discussion of 'professionalism' as a concept and its relevance for activation work.

'Professionalism' in activation work

Twenty years ago, Bovens and Zouridis had already described welfare agencies as 'screen-level' bureaucracies where contacts with citizens largely ran 'through or in the presence of a computer screen' (2002: 177). This was not just as means of storing information but as systems for making decisions by 'entering responses to standardised questions into a computer programme' (Marston, 2006: 91).

For some scholars, the processing of decisions via standardised instruments can denote a form of professional practice *if* such tools encode evidenced-based standards (van Berkel, 2017; van Berkel et al, 2021). Ponnert and Svensson associate such tools with the 'audit society' and the accountability demands of the evidence-based movement in social work 'to demonstrate all the steps that have been taken, to follow manuals and to systematically strive for best practice' (2015: 588). Other scholars are more critical, arguing that standardised decision protocols constrain possibilities for agency by concealing the complexity of cases and filtering discretion through 'a belt of restrictions' (Høybye-Mortensen, 2015: 612). Of further concern is the potential for decision-support systems to pave the way for case managers to be *de*-skilled, replacing 'part of the skill set that a case manager might otherwise need' (Considine et al, 2011: 821). Organisations may then be emboldened to hire workers from a broad range of backgrounds to perform work that previously would have been done by social work (or other allied) professionals. For instance, in their study of the effects of ten years of quasi-marketisation on the frontline delivery of employment services in Australia, Considine and colleagues found that not only had IT systems come to dictate more and more of the work; the people delivering employment services had also become much younger and far less skilled. Over the period 1998 to 2008 the proportion holding a university degree declined from 39 to 24 per cent, the proportion aged under 35 years of age rose from 29 to 42 per cent, and the proportion who were trade union members dropped off a cliff to just 7 per cent (Considine et al, 2015). Put simply, quasi-marketisation had precipitated a de-skilling and de-collectivisation of the frontline workforce that was allied to a routinisation of the case management task.

One way of interpreting such workforce changes is through the concepts of 'controlled' (Noordegraaf, 2015) or 'organisational' (Evetts, 2013) professionalism, which Evetts defines as a discourse of control involving 'the increased standardisation of work procedures' and organisation of work through 'externalised forms of regulation and accountability measures such as target-setting and performance review' (2013: 787). Clearly the intensification of performance measurement feeds into organisational professionalism, although it also encompasses a broader set of dynamics including processes of standardisation and de-skilling.

Organisational professionalism stands opposed to more normative concepts of 'occupational' (Evetts, 2011) or 'pure' (Noordegraaf, 2007: 765) professionalism; models that assume trust in practitioners from both clients and employers, and which are based on 'discretionary judgement and assessment by practitioners of complex cases' (Evetts, 2013: 787). The work of occupational professionals is coordinated through 'collegial authority' (Ponnert and Svensson, 2015: 593) and the cultivation of 'a professional "habitus"' (Noordegraaf, 2015: 191) through training and adherence to occupationally defined codes of conduct. The most proximate examples are the legal and medical professions, although few occupations today constitute professions in this 'classic' (Noordegraaf, 2007: 765) sense. Rather, contemporary occupational life is characterised by varied modes of 'hybrid professionalism' where managerial and occupational systems for coordinating work intersect. Even in expert fields such as medicine, practitioners perform their work through combining 'the managerial tools of the organisation they work in with the disciplinary knowledge of their profession' (Mik-Meyer, 2018: e282).

Notwithstanding the hybrid nature of professionalism today, whether activation work meets the conditions of a profession is doubtful. This is despite the widening of activation to groups of citizens with more differentiated needs and resulting demands on caseworkers to make decisions about increasingly complex cases (Rice, 2017). For this reason, some scholars argue that activation work 'should be organised and managed as professional work' (van Berkel et al, 2021: 2) or even restricted to 'trained social workers ... given the complexity of the employment-services task and needs of clients' (Greer et al, 2017: 110). This is indeed the case in some Nordic countries, where trained social workers continue to account for a sizeable proportion of the employment services workforce (Sadeghi and Fekjær, 2018). This has prompted much debate about the fit between 'activation work' and 'professional social work values' (Nothdurfter, 2016: 435) and whether programmes underpinned by sanctions and conditionality are compatible 'with a professional work (or, at least, social work) repertoire' (van Berkel and van der Aa, 2012: 497).

Yet, in many countries, social workers play only a marginal role in the delivery of activation. Instead, employment services are delivered by workers that van Berkel and colleagues characterise as 'professionals without a profession' (2010: 462). This refers to the fact that they lack any common accredited training, shared vocational association, or 'officially recognized body of knowledge to guide professional decision-making' (van Berkel and van der Aa, 2012: 499). This is especially true in liberal welfare regimes with quasi-market implementation structures (Schram and Silverman, 2012; Greer et al, 2017; O'Sullivan et al, 2021). For instance, in a study of welfare-to-work reforms in Florida, Schram and Silverman found that quasi-marketisation precipitated a shift towards 'a more deskilled' workforce often comprised of ' "recovered" former welfare recipients' (Schram and Silverman, 2012: 131). Indeed, barely *any* of the case managers interviewed for the study were trained in social work or related fields. Instead, their backgrounds were in business and management, or they qualified to work as case managers 'by virtue of their own experience with the system' (Schram and Silverman, 2012: 134). This was also the case among the JobPath staff interviewed for this book. For instance, three of the advisors were recruited to work in JobPath from the Live Register: "I was a customer ... I saw what was going on and I was like 'I could actually do this' and I asked about it. It was in a different office, and I knew the office was opening in my local area ... and I applied, and I got it" (Lisa, JobPath Advisor).

From quasi-marketisation to de-skilling?

So, why does competitive procurement and performance-based contracting tend to produce these effects on the frontline workforce? There are several mechanisms, some of which may be intended while others lead to de-skilling in less direct ways. First, outsourcing enables existing workforces comprised of unionised and professionalised workers to be bypassed in policy implementation. This may be deliberately intended – to weaken labour autonomy and reduce the capacity of social work professionals to thwart workfarist policies (Bredgaard and Larsen, 2007; Larsen, 2013). However, de-skilling may also be driven by more pragmatic considerations of cost containment and 'the uncertainty of contracting' (Greer et al, 2017: 109).

Employment services are labour intensive. Staffing accounts for the lion's share of delivery costs. So, when contracts are awarded on price and payments are mainly based on results, there is an embedded incentive for contractors to cut their staffing costs. First, to be competitive when bidding under conditions of price 'squeezing' (Greer et al, 2017: 111) but second, to reduce the level of financial exposure they need to assume to manage contacts with 'back-ended' (Shutes and Taylor, 2014) payment models. This was one of the reasons why the DSP's decision to replace LES contracts with competitively procured Local Area Employment Services was met with such political resistance. Community sector organisations feared that they "would be out of the game" (Brenda, LES Coordinator) since they would "not be able to compete financially with the big players" (Trevor, LES Coordinator). As a union official explained, with their high fixed costs "in the form of their staff and all of that": "they may not be able to come in as a lowest bidder. And that would be worrying because obviously then you'd have a problem about job retention and conditions and all that" (Annette, Union Official).

Performance-based contracts essentially require providers to fund service delivery upfront: sinking investments into office space, IT infrastructure, and staff against *uncertain* outcome payments. The more leanly and cheaply they can staff their services, the greater their chances of outbidding competitors and reducing the level of risk they need to wear. Within this context, organisations may look to recruit less qualified workers from sectors accustomed to targets rather than experienced professionals with prior sectoral experience – particularly if some tasks can be performed using standardisation tools that

Table 5.4: Use of assessment protocols

Use answers to standard CLIENT CLASSIFICATION (profiling) or checklist when deciding how to work with a client?	JobPath (n = 76)	LES (n = 108)
• Yes	69.7%	46.3%
• No	30.3%	53.7%
p = 0.002 (Fisher's Exact Test)		
Influence of answers to standard set of assessment questions in determining what activities are recommended	**JobPath (n = 74)**	**LES (n = 107)**
• Not at all influential	9.5%	29.0%
• Somewhat influential	37.8%	43.9%
• Quite influential	31.1%	19.6%
• Very influential	21.6%	7.5%
p = 0.001 (Fisher's Exact Test)		

make it easier for 'untrained staff to carry out the task at a much lower cost' (Considine et al, 2015: 57).

There is evidence of organisations adapting to performance-based contracting in this way in the context of Ireland's quasi-market in employment services. As shown in Table 5.4, the use of client profiling instruments was far more widespread among JobPath than LES staff. Indeed, the majority (54 per cent) of LES staff reported that they did *not* use such instruments whereas 70 per cent of the JobPath staff surveyed claim to use client classification instruments when working with clients. Likewise, most (53 per cent) of the JobPath staff surveyed – but only 27 per cent of LES respondents – reported that the answers to standard assessment questions were 'quite' or 'very' influential' in determining what activities they recommended to clients.

In follow-up interviews, JobPath staff elaborated on how they used assessment tools to "try and get the barriers out of" (Liam,

JobPath Advisor) clients; especially during initial appointments, when they would run through questions on "things like literacy levels, computer skills, confidence levels, their attitudes towards learning and education" (Liam, JobPath Advisor). Each JobPath provider had a standardised assessment protocol of some sort that advisors reported using "to bring up the challenges and actions that you have to look at each appointment" (Paula, JobPath Advisor) and to develop progression plans with jobseekers. Indeed, several of the service-users interviewed for this book saw the administering of assessment protocols and completion of PPPs as synonymous:

'I had to fill out this kind of questionnaire … It was all questions about myself; you know, how is my health and general kind of multiple-choice questions … I think it's called the PPP.' (Cormac, service-user, 40s, Limerick)

'They had this PPP, which to me is just all metrics and numbers and graphs. I'm not sure how any of that helps me get a job, but they seemed keen to fill in these forms.' (Padraig, service-user, 40s, Tipperary)

By itself, the use of profiling instruments 'tells us little about the professional or administrative nature of activation work' (van Berkel and van der Aa, 2012: 501). Much depends on *how* they are used and for what purposes. Indeed, such tools could conceivably enhance confidence in the 'professionalism' of activation work if they are used to render the basis of decision-making more transparent and accountable to professional standards rather than personal biases. However, this was not how service-users experienced their use. Rather, their perception was predominantly of a "box-ticking exercise" (Hannah, service-user, 50s, Cork) where the focus was on "only recording the information" (Niall, service-user, 30s, Clare) rather than understanding individual needs. There was a view that advisors "wouldn't have known themselves even" (Niall, service-user, 30s, Clare) what the purpose of the questionaries was:

'The assessment process was you sit beside this guy. He's on a computer. He pulls up a screen with all these boxes to tick. So, it's like, "Can you type?" Tick ... "Do you have clothes to wear to an interview?" ... I just felt a lot of the questions that he was asking, and ticking and ticking and ticking, there is no in-depth talk about what exactly each question entails.' (Siobhan, service-user, 50s, Laois)

'The person who was asking, he didn't seem too sure of what he was doing. He just wanted to get the thing done. And the questions were so ambiguous ... I kept saying, "I don't know. There isn't a yes or no to that one". And he'd say, "Well, we'll just put in this one".' (Laoise, service-user, 50s, Kilkenny)

Occupational fragmentation

Embedded in these criticisms of the use of assessment protocols was a perception that the advisors that service-users' encountered "aren't even qualified themselves" (Ray, service-user, 20s, Offaly) and that the "software system allows anyone to be a consultant" (Sarah, service-user, 40s, Limerick). In interviews, service-users recounted coming across advisors who themselves had "just come off the Dole ... [and who's] only experience had been to go through the process of being on one side of the desk" (Jim, service-user, 40s, Dublin). Some claimed to have applied to become advisors themselves, noting that "the basic requirement ... was a Leaving [High-School] Certificate" (Cormac, service-user, 40s, Limerick).

While these criticisms of the competencies of advisors may have been coloured by service-users' negative experiences of the programme, they resonate with the details of DSP inspection reports released under freedom of information to a group of journalists and researchers. Summarising the types of caseworkers described in the 26 inspection reports they obtained of contractors' offices, Roche and Griffin observe that their backgrounds included 'recruitment, phone shop sales, car sales, and bar work' (2022: 11). The upshot, they argue, is the embedding of 'naturalised ignorance' at the frontline of activation and the absence of any 'basic knowledge, education and training in professional [employment services] casework' (Roche and Griffin, 2022: 11). The survey data collected for the research underpinning this book points to similar concerns about the experience and qualification levels of JobPath frontline staff.

As Table 5.5 shows, the proportion of frontline staff who reported having a university degree was 65 per cent among LES respondents but just 38 per cent among JobPath respondents. Indeed, almost a quarter (23 per cent) of the JobPath staff reported that they had no post-secondary qualification. Moreover, the follow-up interviews suggested that LES staff often had tertiary qualifications in areas directly related to employment guidance. Most of the LES staff who were interviewed (7 out of 10) had worked in employment services for over 20 years. Most had also undertaken formal qualifications in Adult Guidance offered through Maynooth University's Department of Adult and Community Education that included modules on models of guidance and counselling; applied guidance skills; case review; and developing a Quality of Work Life (Department of Adult and Community Education, 2020). Although not a pre-requisite for working in the sector, the course – developed initially in collaboration with FÁS – functioned as a certification of competency and steppingstone to advanced study that appeared to be widely recognised in the field. For instance, one mediator reported that they "did the Maynooth course" before going on to do a Masters in "leadership for the community and public sector" (Michelle, LES Mediator). Another went on to training in "psychotherapy and facilitation" and a subsequent "Masters in Personal and Management Coaching" (Angela, LES Mediator), while a third

Table 5.5: Age, qualification levels, and occupational backgrounds of workers

Age	JobPath (n = 77)	LES (n = 112)
• Under 35	33.8%	3.6%
• 35–44	35.1%	13.4%
• 45–54	19.5%	48.2%
• 55 or over	11.7%	34.8%
$p < 0.001$ (Fisher's Exact Test)		
Union member	**JobPath (n = 77)**	**LES (n = 111)**
• Yes	0.0%	66.7%
$p < 0.001$ (Fisher's Exact Test)		
Highest level of education	**JobPath (n = 77)**	**LES (n = 112)**
• Upper secondary	23.4%	2.7%
• Third-level non-degree	39.0%	31.3%
• Bachelor's degree	31.2%	37.5%
• Postgraduate degree	6.5%	27.7%
• Other	0.0%	0.9%
$p < 0.001$ (Fisher's Exact Test)		
Years worked in welfare or employment services sector	**JobPath (n = 77)**	**LES (n = 112)**
• Less than 1 year	5.2%	2.7%
• 1–5 years	83.1%	10.7%
• More than 5 years	11.7%	86.6%
$p < 0.001$ (Fisher's Exact Test)		
Industry worked in before employment services	**JobPath (n = 77)**	**LES (n = 112)**
• First industry worked in	0.0%	7.1%
• Accommodation and food services (hospitality)	10.4%	0.9%
• Wholesale or retail trade	15.6%	3.6%

(continued)

Table 5.5: Age, qualification levels, and occupational backgrounds of workers (continued)

Age	JobPath (n = 77)	LES (n = 112)
• Personal services	2.6%	0.9%
• Construction or manufacturing	2.6%	7.2%
• Transportation and storage	5.2%	1.8%
• Administrative and support services	16.9%	30.4%
• Health and social work	11.7%	17.9%
• Public administration, defence, or social security	2.6%	3.6%
• Education	2.6%	11.6%
• Information and communication	5.2%	8.0%
• Financial and insurance activities	16.9%	3.6%
• Other	7.8%	3.6%

Source: Adapted from McGann (2022b)

completed "an MSC in Guidance Counselling" after working in addiction services for 17 years (Catherine, LES Mediator).

So, although LES mediators were not professionally trained social workers per se, they resembled a quasi–professionalised workforce to the extent that professional development was valued in their field and there was accredited training available *in a shared body of occupational practice*. Conversely, JobPath advisors reported being trained "very much on the job" (Saoirse, JobPath Advisor) or through "two weeks' training when we started" (Paula, JobPath Advisor). Few had worked in welfare or employment services for more than a few of years. This itself is not surprising, given JobPath only commenced in mid-2015. It does indicate, however, that providers recruited from outside the sector rather than hiring people with prior experience of working with claimants. This is further reflected in the sectors that JobPath and LES staff reported previously having worked in. For instance, just under a third (30 per cent) of the LES staff surveyed reported that they had previously worked in Health and Social Work, or Education – sectors that only 14 per cent of JobPath advisors had come from. A further 30 per cent of LES staff claimed to have previously worked in Administrative and Support Services. This was also a sector that a high proportion (17 per cent) of JobPath staff claimed to have previously worked in, although a further 26 per cent of JobPath staff reported that they had worked in Hospitality or Retail – two of the lowest-paid sectors in the Irish economy (Redmond, 2020) – before moving to employment services.

The Irish data on the impact of quasi-marketisation on the composition of the frontline workforce closely mirrors what Considine and colleagues observed in relation to quasi-marketisation in Australia (Considine and Lewis, 2010; Considine et al, 2015). Compared with LES staff, the workers hired to deliver JobPath were much younger, had lower qualifications, and were entirely de-collectivised (no JobPath staff whatsoever reported union membership). In the Irish case, these changes unfolded over a more compressed period. They were not brought about by temporal shifts in the demography of activation workers or the gradual neoliberal colonisation of the social services workforce. Nor were they the product of skilled professionals leaving the sector out of frustration at increasing levels of managerialism and a growing sense of discrepancy between their 'professional moral frameworks and welfare-to-work' (van Berkel, 2017: 26). This may happen in time. But, for now, the de-skilling of activation workers in Ireland has much more to do with contractors' workforce selection practices in response to the demands of competitive tendering and performance-based contracting.

Whether the qualification levels, experience, and age profile of the JobPath workforce will increase as those organisations become more established remains to be seen. Admittedly, a limitation of the analysis is that the comparison is between street-level workers employed in two relatively new organisations and workers employed in organisations that have existed for 25 years. The JobPath workforce has not had the opportunity to accumulate professional accreditations in the way that the much older and more experienced LES workforce has. That may be the case but the experience of quasi-markets in other liberal welfare regimes does not provide grounds for optimism that this will improve over time. Of all countries, Australia has perhaps the most established welfare-to-work market dating back to the mid-1990s. Yet, the age profile and qualification levels of the frontline workforce have barely changed since the 2000s. For instance, only a quarter of the frontline staff surveyed in 2016 reported holding a university degree while 40 per cent reported being under 35 years of age; almost the same proportions as in 2008 (Lewis et al, 2017). This, combined with the Irish data and what we know from experiences in the US (Schram and Silverman, 2012) and Britain (Greer et al, 2017), would seem to point towards a path dependency in the relationship between marketisation and the de-skilling of activation workers; one that can become 'locked-in' during the initial years of quasi-marketisation and prove stubbornly resistant to change (see Considine et al, 2020a).

From qualifications to dispositions

To round off discussion of the intersection between quasi-marketisation and the politics of professionalism, the chapter concludes with some tentative observations about the potential implications of these occupational dynamics for the types of worldviews and beliefs about the unemployed that case managers may bring to their jobs. For it is well known from previous studies that a key influence on street-level decision-making is the *moral* judgements of deservingness that frontline workers so often make about their individual clients but also broader populations of service-users (Zacka, 2017; Maynard-Moody and Musheno, 2000; McGann et al, 2022). For instance, previous Australian research suggests that frontline workers are more inclined to turn to sanctions and to adopt

REMODELLING AGENCY AT THE STREET-LEVEL

a 'work-first' approach if they believe that most claimants are unemployed through a lack of individual effort rather than circumstances beyond their control (McGann et al, 2020).

The salience of these normative assessments, which are heavily informed by the circulation of welfare discourses both at a policy and organisational level, is further highlighted by Redman and Fletcher's study of the sanctioning practices of Jobcentre Plus advisors in Britain. While 'off-benefit flow' targets fed into the sanctioning of claimants by advisors, so too did the stigmatising power of 'pejorative welfare tropes' as beliefs that claimants were workshy and even gaming the system desensitised advisors to 'the humanity of their caseloads' and permitted them 'to justify punitive working practices which would likely lead to harmful outcomes' (Redman and Fletcher, 2021: 14).

What follows are offered as *tentative* observations to be further explored in future research as the study data are not entirely conclusive on the extent to which the observed differences in normative understandings between JobPath and LES staff reflect differences in their professional identities and occupational backgrounds. However, studies from other jurisdictions offer some evidence that workers' occupational backgrounds may be significant for whether they subscribe to the pathological theories of unemployment underpinning workfarist policies. For instance, research comparing the attitudes of social work professionals with case managers from other backgrounds suggests that the latter are more likely to blame unemployment on jobseekers' lack of effort rather than more structural causes. This has been found to be the case in both Nordic (Kallio et al, 2013) and liberal (McDonald and Marston, 2008) countries.

The Irish survey data reported in Table 5.6 points to similar attitudinal differences between the JobPath and LES frontline staff. When asked which is more often to blame if a person is on benefits, a lack of effort on their part or circumstances beyond their control, a higher proportion of JobPath staff (38 per cent) blamed being on benefits on jobseekers' lack of effort whereas

Table 5.6: Attitudes towards welfare and unemployment

In your opinion, which is more often to blame if a person is on benefits ...?	JobPath (n = 77)	LES (n = 112)	No degree (n = 86)	Degree (n = 102)
1. Lack of effort	2.6%	3.6%	5.8%	1.0%
2.	7.8%	2.7%	5.8%	3.9%
3.	27.3%	20.5%	31.4%	16.7%
4.	33.8%	33.9%	27.9%	38.2%
5.	18.2%	16.1%	17.4%	16.7%
6.	7.8%	13.4%	7.0%	14.7%
7. Circumstances beyond their control	2.6%	9.8%	4.7%	8.8.%
Mann-Whitney U-test	Z = 2.121 p = 0.034		Z = -2.944 p = 0.003	
Estimated percentage of claimants who would rather be on benefits than work ...	**JobPath** (n = 77)	**LES** (n = 109)	**No Degree** (n = 85)	**Degree** (n = 100)
Mean	38.5%	32.6%	39.9%	30.1%
Mann-Whitney U-test	Z = -2.2 p = 0.032		Z = -2.994 p = 0.003	
Whether there should be more government spending on benefits for unemployed people	**JobPath** (n = 77)	**LES** (n = 111)	**No Degree** (n = 85)	**Degree** (n = 102)
• Strongly agree	6.5%	15.3%	7.1%	15.7%
• Agree	14.3%	26.1%	23.5%	19.6%
• Neither	18.2%	26.1%	24.7%	20.6%
• Disagree	48.1%	26.1%	35.3%	35.3%
• Strongly disagree	13.0%	6.3%	9.4%	8.8%
Mann-Whitney U-test	Z = -3.8 p < 0.001		Z = -0.673 p = 0.502	

just 27 per cent of LES staff reported this view. Similarly, when asked to estimate the proportion of claimants 'who would rather be on benefits than work to support themselves and their families', JobPath respondents gave a mean estimate of just under 39 per cent whereas LES respondents, on average, estimated this proportion to be under 33 per cent. Finally, when asked whether they felt there should be more government spending on benefits for unemployed people than currently, 61 per cent of JobPath respondents disagreed or strongly disagreed with increasing spending on benefits. Conversely, a higher proportion of LES respondents were in favour (41 per cent) of increasing spending on benefits than were opposed (32 per cent).

Put simply, JobPath staffs' normative understandings of welfare were more in line with the pathological theories of unemployment and discourses of welfare dependency underpinning workfarist activation than those of LES staff. This was also reflected in the interview data, with most of the JobPath staff citing claimants' lack of motivation and the relative generosity of payments as significant barriers to employment. While a small number of LES mediators also held such views, they were not as widely expressed as among the JobPath staff who frequently articulated the view that a significant proportion of claimants were unmotivated to work:

'Some people need a bit of a; I wouldn't call it a kick up the ass, but they need a bit of a kind of rude awakening … Generally, I'd say younger people, they need a bit of kind of an awakening that they can't always stay like this forever. "You're moving into your late 20s, or 30s … You can't be sitting be home with mammy all the time … It's time to grow up".' (Liam, JobPath Advisor)

'I would have had family who would have been on social welfare, and I'm looking and I'm going "You are not bothering, you are not bothering. You don't have to get out of bed except for the day that you collect your money".' (Trish, JobPath Manager)

'You can get into a rut on Jobseeker's Allowance … where you just think "Ah sure look, grand I'm getting my whatever payment a week, and my rent is paid and

all" ... I do see it as across the board.' (Joanna, JobPath
Employer liaison and ex-advisor)

Whether these attitudinal differences in LES and JobPath
workers' beliefs about welfare and unemployment reflect
differences in their 'professional' backgrounds is difficult to say.
Although the data in Table 5.6 does show that respondents'
answers to these attitudinal questions differed depending on
whether they held a university degree. Other than respondents'
attitudes towards increasing spending on benefits, those who
reported holding a degree were more inclined towards structural
rather than behavioural explanations of unemployment. For
instance, among those with a university degree, the mean
estimated proportion of claimants who would rather be on
benefits than work was just 30 per cent compared with an
estimate of almost 40 per cent among those without a degree.
Similarly, only 21 per cent of frontline staff with a degree
reported that a lack of effort was the reason why people were on
benefits compared with 43 per cent of those without a degree.

Qualification levels, of course, are not synonymous with
occupational background (respondents' previous occupations
were too varied to meaningfully compare whether this was
associated with attitudinal differences). Although the interview
data did suggest that LES workers' degrees were typically
associated with undertaking study in employment guidance,
adult counselling, and other fields related to working with
the long-term unemployed. To this extent, the differences in
frontline workers' qualification levels likely tracked differences
in their professional backgrounds. In other words, it is not
higher qualifications per se that potentially inoculates frontline
workers against pathological theories of unemployment but
accredited training in fields closely associated with employment
guidance and counselling. Nonetheless, further work is needed
to examine this relationship between street-level workers'
occupational backgrounds and their normative understandings
of unemployment more conclusively.

SIX

Conclusion

This book offers a detailed study of the 'double dynamics' (Newman, 2007) of activation in Ireland that speaks to wider intersections between the workfarist turn in activation policy and the governance turn towards marketisation in welfare administration. In so doing, it illuminates the *political* effects of governance reforms to underscore that 'the practical is political' (Brodkin, 2013a: 32). Specially, the book tries to explicate the mechanisms by which marketisation reinforces and accentuates the activation of claimants in more demanding, workfarist ways, while also tracing the shifting sectoral division of welfare in Ireland and the gaining ascendency of the market as the means for deploying the commodifying power of the state.

The core thread of the book is the logic of commodification underpinning both the administrative and policy tracks of contemporary welfare reform. Activation policies deploy conduct conditionality to motivate un(der)employed people to sell their labour on the open market. Quasi-marketisation tries to ensure that providers deliver upon this project of activation by, in turn, further converting non-employed labour into a fungible commodity that can be acquired through a competitive tender, polished, and sold on for profit. Importantly, the two forms of commodification work in tandem: conceiving of their clients in commodity terms orients frontline workers towards getting jobseekers into work as quickly as possible rather than supporting them to gain the qualifications and experience needed to achieve longer-term employment goals. To this extent, the book builds on the concept of 'double activation' as an analytical lens for scrutinising the dynamic interaction between the two tracks of welfare reform, surfacing how welfare reform proceeds 'as a productive project of discipline' that applies to delivery agents 'as much as the poor themselves' (Soss et al, 2011a: 296).

The Irish case

This is far from the first study of the impact of marketisation on the delivery of welfare-to-work. It owes much to the rich body of work that has preceded it by a range of scholars from Australia, Britain, Denmark, Germany, the Netherlands, and United States among other countries (for example Considine, 2001; Bredgaard and Larsen, 2007; Brodkin, 2011; Soss et al, 2011a; van Berkel, 2013, 2017; Larsen and Wright, 2014; Considine et al, 2015; Fuertes and Lindsay, 2016; Greer et al, 2017; O'Sullivan et al, 2021). Where the book breaks new ground is in offering an original study of the delivery of activation by street-level organisations in Ireland and in *synchronously comparing* the frontline delivery of welfare-to-work under different governance conditions.

The pluri-governance approach to commissioning employment services that operated in Ireland from 2015 to 2022 afforded an almost unique opportunity to control for 'policy noise'. By contrast, previous studies of the connections between activation practices and governance reforms have either relied on single case studies of implementation by market providers or evaluated the impact of market governance by tracking changes in delivery over time (before and after various marketisation reforms). The challenge is that marketisation reforms seldom happen in isolation from substantive changes in social security policy. Indeed, it is precisely this confluence of administrative and policy reforms that double activation addresses. This makes it inherently difficult to disentangle whether the observed changes in frontline practice are produced by substantive policy changes filtering down to the street-level, or whether they are rooted in the instruments of administrative governance. The research behind this book has been able to overcome this issue to an extent because of how the Irish Government originally introduced quasi-marketisation; not as a means for reconfiguring all employment services but as an appendage to a pre-existing network of LES. The result was two parallel services for the long-term unemployed co-existing in policy space and time. Not only were they targeted at the same cohorts of claimants; they were contracted by the very same unit of the DSP. The principal, policy settings, and policy objectives were the same, but the delivery agents and governance instruments used to steer implementation were altogether different.

The Irish case filters out the policy noise that often clouds studies of double activation. Claims about the effects of market governance on the nature of frontline delivery can consequently be put to the test in new ways, and in a context where commitment to activation reform has historically been weak. In some ways Ireland provides a 'least likely' case – at least among liberal welfare regimes – for testing the points of intersection between workfare and quasi-marketisation. It was an outlier not just among liberal welfare states but across OECD countries as far as the use of sanctions and conditionality goes. Support for the welfare state was comparatively high for a liberal regime, albeit one with 'a "kinder and gentler" political culture' (Hick and Murphy, 2021: 314), and active labour market spending was predominantly oriented around training, work experience, and job creation programmes.

All this suggests that Ireland should not have been an especially fertile ground for cultivating workfarist practices and that the effects of market governance on skewing the delivery of welfare-to-work in more demanding ways would potentially be quite muted. Yet, the analysis in Chapter Four showed that this was not the case. While Ireland's JobPath might not be especially workfarist compared with welfare-to-work markets in other liberal regimes, Ireland's quasi-market did mark a significant departure way from the human capital development orientation that had gone before, and which LES continued to aspire towards. Coupled with the already mentioned body of international evidence, this suggests that the connections between workfare policy practices and market governance implementation structures are far from ad hoc but systematic and deeply inscribed in the dynamics of competitive tendering, price-bidding, and outcomes-based contracting. A key contribution of this book has been to isolate these points of intersection – conceptually and empirically – and to give an account of their underlying dynamics.

Connecting workfare and marketisation

Conceptually, the book unpacks the underlying theories of human motivation and commodification of the unemployed, shared by proponents of workfare and quasi-marketisation. Chapter Three positions quasi-marketisation as a form of *hyper-commodification* of the unemployed – identifying how allocating employment services through competitive tendering and outcomes-based contracting involves organising claimants into lots to be bid for, acquired, and sold on for profit by contractors. To the extent that workfare policies constitute strategies of administrative re-commodification, quasi-marketisation involves the state-sanctioned multiplication of how profit can be extracted from surplus labour, giving rise to a welfare-to-work system replete with 'affirmative sites of commodification' (Soss et al, 2011a: 297).

Chapter Three also draws out the parallels between the pathological theory of unemployment motivating workfare, and the assumptions made by proponents of quasi-marketisation about the motivations of service workers. In each case there is a presumption that welfare and administrative subjects will fall idle if not externally incentivised (through threats of sanctions, performance measurement or outcomes-based payments) to pursue defined objectives. Thus, claimants are configured 'as individual units of (paid) labour which need to be financially incentivised to sell their labour, and service providers as market agents which need to be financially incentivised to place people in paid work' (Shutes and Taylor, 2014: 217). Yet the means deployed to incentivise service providers largely depends on a further layer of claimant commodification; transfiguring welfare recipients into commodities that can be traded into jobs for outcome payments. In a very real sense, it involves the unemployed "being sold by the state" (Hannah, service-user, 50s, Cork) as several of those interviewed for this book were all too aware.

Chapter Four demonstrates that the intersection between workfare and quasi-marketisation is not just theoretical but plays out in practice in terms of reorienting the delivery of employment services away from enabling supports towards a more demanding model of activation. This was reflected in the apparent willingness of JobPath staff to report clients for breaching mutual commitments – especially in circumstances concerning job-search conditionality – and in the greater demands that were made on service-users' time to more frequently attend appointments and 'job-search sessions' at offices. 'Enabling' support was essentially limited to job-search training workshops on preparing CVs, cover letters, and interview techniques rather than encouraging participation in education, work experience, or substantive training. In short, the locus of support was on increasing the intensity and effectiveness of claimants' job-searching whereas there was evidence that LES placed a greater priority on human capital development as the route to employability. This was consistent across the frontline survey data and the experiences of the two employment services reported by service-users.

Beyond demonstrating the connection – conceptually and empirically – between the marketisation of employment services and the shift towards a more conditional and demanding model of activation, the book evaluates *how* the agency of street-level workers is remodelled by the processes of competitive tendering, price-bidding, and outcomes-based contracting inherent to market governance. This is key to understanding the mechanisms by which macro-level governance reforms in service commissioning cascade down to change micro-level, street-level practices. Behind the 'black box' of frontline delivery is an organisational toolkit of managerialism and performance measurement that is in turn shaped by the workforce selection practices of providers.

Figure 6.1 models these dynamics, discussed in Chapter Five, of the *politics of discretion* and *politics of professionalism* produced by quasi-marketisation. In terms of the politics of discretion, quasi-marketisation is associated with the application of more intensive regimes of performance measurement and monitoring by organisational managers who are concerned with the delivery of payable results and their staff's compliance with contractual terms. The upshot is an emphasis on 'performing performance' that spills into advisors "giving [jobseekers] a silly task for the sake of it" (Carl, JobPath Advisor) just so that they are 'seen' to be activating their clients in the administrative footprints recorded on information management systems. However, it is not just the use of targets and performance measurement per se that recasts how street-level workers exercise their administrative discretion. Indeed, LES staff equally reported being subject to targets and performance monitoring albeit not the same frequency or intensity of supervisory oversight as JobPath staff. Rather, the key aspect of how quasi-marketisation transforms the politics of discretion appeared to be the degree to which the frontline staff working under conditions of market governance internalised the commodity value of their own work performance. It was this attentiveness to whether their actions with clients

Figure 6.1: How quasi-marketisation reconfigures organisational conditions and agency of street-level workers to reshape frontline practice

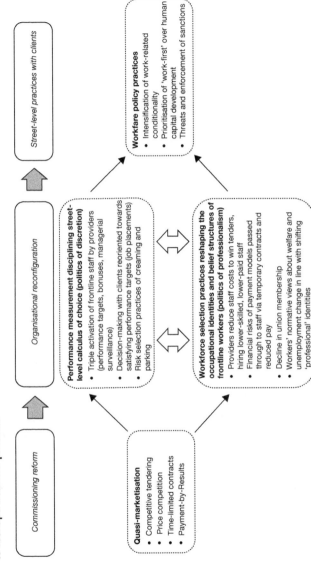

Source: Adapted from McGann (2022b)

would generate a payable employment outcome, and their awareness that the income they generated for the organisation was being actively monitored, that was most associated with a workfarist disposition towards prioritising rapid job placement over human capital development. Put simply, the hyper-commodification of claimants inherent to quasi-marketisation intensified the administrative re-commodification of claimants animating the social policy turn towards activation.

A second key dynamic by which quasi-marketisation restructures the nature of administrative agency in policy delivery is through providers' workforce selection practices and the politics of professionalism. Allocating responsibility for the delivery of employment services through competitive tendering and results-based payment models generates embedded incentives for providers to cut costs. They must do so to be competitive on price when bidding for contracts and to minimise their financial exposure on contracts that render their revenues contingent upon the volumes and duration of job placements they can secure. These revenues are far from certain when the proportion of the caseload that progresses to 52 weeks or more of full-time employment is only about 7 per cent (Oireachtas Committee, 2021: 8). Because staffing is among the most significant cost facing contractors, there is an understandable temptation for providers to recruit inexperienced workers rather than more costly trained professionals. However, to do so, they must routinise as much of the case management task as possible through developing standardised procedural guidelines and assessment protocols that can be easily followed to arrive at recommended but somewhat generic courses of action. The upshot, as Greer and colleagues observe in their comparative study of marketisation in Denmark, Germany, and Britain, is that the resources needed to staff the frontline with qualified professionals are siphoned 'out of services ... and the standardisation of services that this requires drains the capacity of providers to innovate' (2017: 141).

Chapter Five documents robust evidence showing this has been the case also in Ireland. The caseworkers delivering the pre-existing network of LES resemble quasi-professionals. They are mostly unionised, with degree-level qualifications in fields such as employment guidance, career counselling, and community development. The JobPath staff, by contrast, are much more emblematic of the ambiguous status of activation workers as 'professionals without a profession' (van Berkel et al, 2010). They come from a plethora of low-paid occupational backgrounds and only a minority have degree-level qualifications. Perhaps most significant of all is the fact that they are an entirely de-collectivised workforce. The low-skilled status of the JobPath workforce is further reflected in the extent to which they rely on processing case decisions through standardised assessment protocols and client profiling instruments. The overriding experience of service-users is therefore almost inevitably of a "very impersonal" (Beatrice, service-user, 30s, Dublin), "cut and pasted" (Keven, service-user, 50s, Tipperary), "run of the mill" (Shay, service-user, 20s, Waterford) and "blanket, one-size-fits-all" (Anna, service-user, 30s, Dublin) approach. "It's like a factory" (Megan, service-user, 40s, Cavan) where jobseekers are the inputs to an assembly line operated by frontline staff following pre-determined workflows.

This connection between quasi-marketisation and the politics of professionalism in activation work is perhaps not as widely remarked upon in the literature as the connection between marketisation and the disciplining of discretion via targets and performance measurement. But it is no less significant to understanding how instruments of market governance reconfigure the agency of street-level workers. Quasi-marketisation transforms agency in policy delivery by not only changing the managerial and performance regimes under which street-level workers' exercise their discretion. It also fundamentally dislodges *who* holds that agency in the first place, shifting the types of professional identities, occupational experiences, and even moral belief structures that imbue the delivery of welfare-to-work. There is accumulated evidence of this occurring in Australia, the US, Britain, and now Ireland such that it can legitimately be asked whether the project of advancing professionalism in activation work is incompatible with the creation and continuation of markets in welfare-to-work. Perhaps this is too bold a claim, but a fundamental trade-off needs to be faced between the pursuit of cost efficiency and quality in frontline service delivery (see Greer et al, 2017). The purported double dividend of low-lost, high-quality employment services is a mirage that has all too often captivated the agenda of welfare reform.

In identifying these two dynamics tracing workfare policy practices to instruments of market governance, it should not be presumed that these are entirely discrete mechanisms. To the contrary, the intensification of managerialism and performance measurement within delivery organisations is likely to go hand in glove with the de-skilling of frontline staff. This is not least because systems of managerial scrutiny and performance measurement will be easier to implement in the context of a less experienced, lower qualified, and non-unionised workforce. To this extent, the politics of discretion and the politics of professionalism are reinforcing. Each begets the other, and each begets a more demanding workfarist orientation.

Does workfare work?

What has yet to be addressed in any detail is the extent to which workfarist activation works. Behind the book's critique of activation's double dynamics is an implicit assumption that what is produced when workfare meets marketisation is detrimental to the interests of the long-term unemployed. The experiences reported by the service-users interviewed for this book certainly give credence to this assumption. But that is a topic for another day. To satisfactorily address it would require detailed engagement with a now vast literature on the evaluation of active labour market policies (for example Kluve, 2010; Martin, 2015; Card et al, 2018), as well as the many critiques of the prevailing modalities and approaches used to evaluate the 'success' of different activation measures (see Dall and Danneris, 2019). All that can be offered here is a cursory glimpse of some key lines of enquiry. These concern important debates about the parameters of evaluation that raise critical questions about the purpose of activation and who programmes are targeted toward.

The selection of *what* to measure is a political choice with highly significant ramifications for how policies are evaluated. Should success be judged by how many people are moved off benefits; by how many find employment; by the quality of employment transitions in terms of sustainability and earnings; or by the impact on people's wellbeing more broadly conceived? Each of these are very different measures, so the 'success' of programmes will look very different depending on the choice of measure. When the preferred measures of success are off-benefit rates and the speed at which people return to work the outcomes of programmes characterised by job-search services and sanctions appear quite good. However, exiting welfare is not synonymous with entering employment and even then, the aim of employment services 'should not only be to get people off benefits and into work, but also to help them access "quality" jobs' (Martin, 2015: 22). To this extent, a critique of workfare models is not only that they result in many people being 'activated to take low-wage jobs ... which may not lift them and their families permanently out of poverty' (Martin, 2015: 22). They can also give rise to people exiting welfare caseloads 'to destinations unrelated to work' (Loopstra et al, 2015: 11).

This may be to other payments with less onerous conduct conditions, such as disability payments, as was the case for one former JobPath participant interviewed for this book. Having already completed a year on JobPath, Cormac explained that he was driven to apply for illness benefit to avoid another referral to JobPath:

'I went to my doctor to write me a letter to basically put me on an illness benefit, to get me out of going ... With [JobPath], going in and out every week and feeling this kind of us and them approach, it would not help anyone's mental health either. I found I was just going in and doing a pointless thing of job-searching week-in, week-out and I did not fancy going through the whole thing again.' (Cormac, service-user, 40s, Limerick)

In other cases, people may forgo welfare altogether, as happened in the case of Emer. To avoid a second referral to JobPath, she signed off the payment she was receiving as a supplement to her part-time job even though there was no increase in her work hours:

'I got another letter from JobPath to go back into it again for another year. And I made the choice then, because I just knew it would just bring me down, so I came off the two days Social Welfare ... I didn't want to put my head into another place that was going to bring me down ... it was kind of like the money against your mental health.' (Emer, service use, 40s, Dublin)

Workfare programmes may reduce welfare caseloads and accelerate the speed at which some people return to employment. But they can also lead to hidden unemployment and in-work poverty (Arni et al, 2013; Seikel and Spannagel, 2018), as in the examples of Cormac and Emer who also articulated saliant concerns about the potential impacts of participation on their mental health. Here, Carter and Whitworth argue for the importance of differentiating between the 'process wellbeing' and 'outcome wellbeing' effects of activation. While the psychological benefits of employment are frequently invoked to justify mandatory activation, 'the *process* of participation in activation schemes can also affect claimants' wellbeing *in and of itself*' (Carter and Whitworth, 2017: 798); and not always positively. Indeed, Carter and Whitworth's research on the wellbeing of Work Programme participants suggests 'a fairly bleak picture' where participants are 'no better off … [and] quite possibly worse off' (2017: 811) in terms of their wellbeing than unemployed people not participating in the programme.

Beyond the problem of what to measure, there is also the question of how long the *duration* of measurement should be. This is especially pertinent when comparing the outcomes of job-search services and sanctions approaches against human capital approaches. The literature comparing the two main activation approaches tends to find that 'job-search assistance and sanctions' approaches have large short-term effects on employment participation over one to two years but that human capital approaches tend to have more positive effects 'in the medium or longer run' (three to five years) (Card et al, 2018: 31). For instance, an Australian study drawing on panel data from over 6,000 unemployed people found that, over the long run, people who were subject to mutual obligation moved into 'lower quality jobs' (Gerards and Welters, 2022: 957) in terms of earnings and hours than similarly matched cohorts without job-search conditionality. In a review of over 90 studies on the impacts of sanctions, Pattaro and colleagues similarly found that although studies consistently report positive short-term impacts on employment, sanctions are also associated 'with a range of adverse impacts in terms of worsening job quality and stability in the longer term' (2022: 35) as well as higher exists to non-employment.

In short, the evaluation literature is far from conclusive. Workfare models seem effective when outcomes are measured over a shorter duration and in terms of 'off-benefit' rates or speed to employment. In this respect, an econometric evaluation of JobPath found that the programme was 'effective in supporting long-term unemployed people secure work' (DEASP, 2019: x) with the rate of employment being 20 per cent higher in 2017 among people who had participated in JobPath the previous year, compared to similarly matched cohorts who did not participate in JobPath or indeed *any* employment service. However, the results of workfare programmes appear less impressive when judged over a longer period and by other measures. The cohorts towards which programmes are targeted are also key to understanding their results. The outcomes that programmes achieve for participants with few barriers to employment other than a lack of work cannot be assumed to translate to other cohorts with multiple and complex needs. Nor can it be assumed that what works in one national or labour market context will also work in another. To this extent, a key problem with the prevailing econometric approaches to evaluating activation programmes is their tendency to treat the problem of unemployment, and the interventions addressing it, 'as standardisable, constant, and measurable' (Dall and Danneris, 2019: 585).

Why is it then that governments across countries, including Ireland, have become so enthralled by workfarist policies? The answer most likely lies in politics and ideology. The unemployed are a politically weak group. Their small number poses little threat at the ballot box while there is political currency to be made in politicians appearing tough on welfare and appealing to tropes of 'lifters, not leaners' and 'strivers, not skivers'. The narrative that a significant proportion of people are claiming benefits due to the low-intensity and ineffectiveness of their job-searching also conveniently conceals the structural causes of unemployment, and policymakers' failure to address them. To this extent, political commitment to workfare is driven more by 'gesture politics' (Power et al, 2022: 8) than empirical evidence; a form of political dog-whistling in which claimants are the victims of not just economic but political commodification.

References

Adkins, L. (2017) 'Disobedient workers, the law and the making of unemployment markets', *Sociology*, 51(2): 290–305.

Arni, P., Lalive, R., and van Ours, J. (2013) 'How effective are unemployment benefit sanctions? Looking beyond unemployment exit', *Journal of Applied Econometrics*, 28: 1153–78.

Asselineau, A., Grolleau, G., and Mzoughi, N. (2022) 'A good servant but a poor master: the side effects of numbers and metrics', *Administration and Society*, 54(5): 971–91.

Behn, R.D. (2003) 'Why measure performance? Different purposes require different measures', *Public Administration Review*, 63(5): 586–606.

Bekker, S. and Mailand, M. (2019) 'The European flexicurity concept and the Dutch and Danish flexicurity models: How have they managed the Great Recession?', *Social Policy and Administration*, 53(1): 142–55.

Benish, A. and Mattei, P. (2020) 'Accountability and hybridity in welfare governance', *Public Administration*, 98(2): 281–90.

Bennett, H. (2017) 'Re-examining British welfare-to-work contracting using a transaction cost perspective', *Journal of Social Policy*, 46(1): 129–48.

Boland, T. and Griffin, R. (2018) 'The purgatorial ethic and the spirit of welfare', *Journal of Classical Sociology*, 18(2): 87–103.

Boland, T. and Griffin, R. (2021) *The Reformation of Welfare: The New Faith of the Labour Market*. Bristol: Policy Press.

Boland, T., Doyle, K., and Griffin, R. (2022) 'Passing stigma: negotiations of welfare categories as street-level governmentality', *Social Policy and Society*, 21(4): 657–67.

Bonoli, G. (2010) 'The political economy of active labour market policy', *Politics and Society*, 38(4): 435–57.

Bovens, M. and Zouridis, S. (2002) 'From street-level to system-level bureaucracies: how information and communication technology is transforming administrative discretion', *Public Administration Review*, 62(2): 174–84.

Bredgaard, T. and Larsen, F. (2007) 'Implementing public employment policy: What happens when non-public agencies take over?', *International Journal of Sociology and Social Policy*, 27(7/8): 287–300.

Brodkin E.Z. (1997) 'Inside the welfare contract: Discretion and accountability in state welfare administration', *Social Service Review*, 71(1): 1–33.

Brodkin, E.Z. (2008) 'Accountability in street-level organisations', *International Journal of Public Administration*, 31(3): 317–36.

Brodkin, E.Z. (2011) 'Policy work: Street-level organisations under new managerialism', *Journal of Public Administration Research and Theory*, 21(supplement): i253–77.

Brodkin, E.Z. (2013a) 'Street-level organisations and the welfare state', in E.Z. Brodkin and G. Marston (eds) *Work and the Welfare State: Street-Level Organisations and Workfare Politics*. Copenhagen: Djorf, pp 17–36.

Brodkin, E.Z. (2013b) 'Work and the welfare state', in E.Z. Brodkin and G. Marston (eds) *Work and the Welfare State: Street-Level Organisations and Workfare Politics*. Copenhagen: Djorf, pp 3–16.

Brodkin, E.Z. (2013c) 'Work and the welfare state reconsidered', in E.Z. Brodkin and G. Marston (eds) *Work and the Welfare State: Street-Level Organisations and Workfare Politics*. Copenhagen: Djorf, pp 271–81.

Brodkin, E.Z. (2015) 'Street-level organisations and the "real world" of workfare: Lessons from the US', *Social Work and Society*, 13(1): 1–16.

REFERENCES

Brodkin, E.Z. (2017) 'The ethnographic turn in political science: Reflections on the state of the art', *Political Science and Politics*, 50(1): 131–34.

Card, D., Kluve, J., and Weber, A. (2018) 'What works? A meta-analysis of recent active labour market program evaluations', *Journal of the European Economic Association*, 16(3): 894–31.

Carter, E. and Whitworth, A. (2015) 'Creaming and parking in quasi-marketised welfare-to-work schemes: Designed out of or designed into the UK Work Programme?', *Journal of Social Policy*, 44(2): 277–96.

Carter, E. and Whitworth, A. (2017) 'Work activation regimes and well-being of unemployed people: Rhetoric, risk and reality of quasi-marketization in the UK Work Programme', *Social Policy and Administration*, 51(5): 796–816.

Caswell, D. and Høybye-Mortensen, M. (2015) 'Responses from the frontline: How organisations and street-level bureaucrats deal with economic sanctions', *European Journal of Social Security*, 1(1): 31–51.

Caswell, D. and Larsen, F. (2017) 'Frontline work in Danish activation policies', in R. van Berkel, D. Caswell, P. Kupka, and F. Larsen (eds) *Frontline Delivery of Welfare-to-Work Policies in Europe*. New York: Routledge, pp 163–80.

Caswell, D., Marston, G., and Larsen, J.E. (2010) 'Unemployed citizen or "at risk" client? Classification systems and employment services in Denmark and Australia', *Critical Social Policy*, 30(3): 384–404.

Caswell, D., Kupka, P., Larsen, F., and van Berkel, R. (2017) 'The frontline delivery of welfare-to-work in context', in R. van Berkel, D. Caswell, P. Kupka and F. Larsen (eds) *Frontline Delivery of Welfare-to-Work Policies in Europe*. New York: Routledge, pp 1–11.

Charlesworth, S.J. (2000) *A Phenomenology of Working-Class Experience*. Cambridge: Cambridge University Press.

Collins, M. and Murphy, M.P. (2016) 'Activation: solving unemployment or supporting a low-pay economy?', in F. Dukelow and M.P. Murphy (eds) *The Irish Welfare State in the Twenty-First Century: Challenges and Change*. London: Palgrave Macmillan, pp 67–92.

Collins, M. and Murphy, M.P. (2021) 'The political economy of work and welfare', in D. Farrell and N. Hardiman (eds) *The Oxford Handbook of Irish Politics*. Oxford: Oxford University Press, pp 423–44.

Committee of Public Accounts (PAC) (2021) *Examination of the 2019 Appropriation Account for Vote 37*. Dublin: Houses of the Oireachtas.

Considine, M. (2001) *Enterprising States: The Public Management of Welfare-to-Work*. Cambridge: Cambridge University Press.

Considine, M. and Lewis, J.M. (2003) 'Bureaucracy, network, or enterprise? Comparing the models of governance in Australia, Britain, the Netherlands, and New Zealand', *Public Administration Review*, 63(2): 131–40.

Considine, M. and Lewis, J.M. (2010) 'Front-line work in employment services after ten years of new public management reform: Governance and activation in Australia, the Netherlands and the UK', *European Journal of Social Security*, 12(4): 357–70.

Considine, M., Lewis, J.M., and O'Sullivan, S. (2011) 'Quasi-markets and service delivery flexibility following a decade of employment assistance reform in Australia', *Journal of Social Policy*, 40(4): 811–33.

Considine, M., Lewis, J.M., O'Sullivan, S., and Sols, E. (2015) *Getting Welfare to Work: Street-Level Governance in Australia, the UK, and the Netherlands*. Oxford: Oxford University Press.

Considine, M., O'Sullivan, S., McGann, M., and Nguyen, P. (2020a) 'Locked-in or locked-out: Can a public services market really change?', *Journal of Social Policy*, 49(4): 850–71.

Considine, M., O'Sullivan, S., McGann, M., and Nguyen, P. (2020b) 'Contracting personalization by results: Comparing marketisation reforms in the UK and Australia', *Public Administration*, 98(4): 873–90.

Cousins, M. (1997) 'Ireland's place in the worlds of welfare capitalism', *Journal of European Social Policy*, 7(3): 223–35.

Cousins, M. (2019) 'Welfare conditionality in the Republic of Ireland after the Great Recession', *Journal of Social Security Law*, 26(1): 30–41.

Dáil Éireann (2019a) JobPath data, 22 January 2019. Available at: https://www.oireachtas.ie/en/debates/question/2019-01-22/655/#pq-answers-655 [accessed 22 January 2020].

Dáil Éireann (2019b) Social welfare schemes data, 17 December 2019. Available at: https://www.oireachtas.ie/en/debates/question/2019-12-17/695/#pq-answers-695 [accessed 29 October 2021].

Dáil Éireann (2021) Employment support services: private members' motion, 30 November 2021. Available at: https://www.oireachtas.ie/en/debates/debate/dail/2021-11-30/19/ [accessed 16 March 2022].

Dall, T. and Danneris, S. (2019) 'Reconsidering "what works" in welfare-to-work with the vulnerable unemployed: The potential of relational causality as an alternative approach', *Social Policy and Society*, 18(4): 583–96.

Daly, M. and Yeates, N. (2003) 'Common origins, different paths: Adaptation and change in social security in Britain and Ireland', *Policy and Politics*, 31(1): 85–97.

de La Porte, C. and Jacobsson, K. (2012) 'Social investment or recommodification? Assessing the employment policies of the EU member states', in N. Morel and B. Palier (eds) *Towards a Social Investment State? Ideas, Policies and Challenges*. Bristol: Policy Press.

Dean, H. (2003) 'Re-conceptualising welfare-to-work for people with multiple problems and needs', *Journal of Social Policy*, 32(3): 441–59.

Dean, H. (2012) 'The ethical deficit of the United Kingdom's proposed Universal Credit: Pimping the precariat?', *The Political Quarterly*, 83(2): 353–59.

Department of Adult and Community Education (2020) Certificate of Adult Guidance Theory and Practice. Available at: https://www.maynoothuniversity.ie/adult- [accessed 11 May 2022].

Department of Employment Affairs and Social Protection (DEASP) (2016) Taoiseach, Tánaiste and Education Minister launch Pathways to Work 2016–2020. Available at: https://www.gov.ie/en/press-release/e07f10-taoiseach-tanaiste-and-education-minister-launch-pathways-to-work-20/ [accessed 21 April 2020].

Department of Employment Affairs and Social Protection (DEASP) (2019) *Evaluation of JobPath outcomes for Q1 2016 participants*. Dublin: DEASP.

Department of Public Expenditure and Reform (DPER) (2014) *Public Sector Reform Plan 2014–2016*. Dublin: DPER.

Department of Social Protection (DSP) (2021a) Opening Statement to the Joint Oireachtas Committee on Social Protection, Community and Rural Development and the Islands, 27 September 2021. Available at: https://data.oireachtas.ie/ie/oireachtas/committee/dail/33/joint_committee_on_social_protection_community_and_rural_development_and_the_islands/submissions/2021/2021-09-29_opening-statement-chris-kane-principal-officer-department-of-social-protection_en.pdf [accessed 25 June 2022]

Department of Social Protection (DSP) (2021b) Request for tender for the provision of a Regional Employment Service. Available at: https://irl.eu-supply.com/ctm/Supplier/PublicPurchase/187298/0/0?returnUrl=&b=ETENDERS_SIMPLE [accessed 30 June 2021].

Department of Social Protection (DSP) (2022a) Minister Humphreys announces outcome of the procurement for new nationwide Intreo Partner Employment Services. Available at: https://www.gov.ie/en/press-release/bb149-minister-humphreys-announces-outcome-of-the-procurement-for-new-nationwide-intreo-partner-employment-services/ [accessed 18 October 2022].

Department of Social Protection (DSP) (2022b) Request for tender for the Provision of an Intreo Partner National Employment Service. Available at: https://irl.eu-supply.com/app/rfq/publicpurchase_docs.asp?PID=208827&LID=237813&AllowPrint=1 [accessed 18 October 2022].

Dias, J.J. and Maynard-Moody, S. (2007) 'For-profit welfare: Contracts, conflicts, and the performance paradox', *Journal of Public Administration Research and Theory*, 17(2): 189–211.

Dingeldey, I. (2007) 'Between workfare and enablement? The different paths to transformation of the welfare state: A comparative analysis of activating labour market policies', *European Journal of Political Research*, 46(6): 823–51.

Dukelow, F. (2015) '"Pushing against an open door": Reinforcing the neo-liberal policy paradigm in Ireland and the impact of EU intrusion', *Comparative European Politics*, 13(1): 93–111.

Dukelow, F. (2021) 'Sacrificial citizens? Activation and retrenchment in Ireland's political economy', *Administration*, 69(2): 43–65.

Dukelow, F. and Considine, M. (2014a) 'Between retrenchment and recalibration: The impact of austerity on the Irish social protection system', *Journal of Sociology and Social Welfare*, 41(1): 55–72.

Dukelow, F. and Considine, M. (2014b) 'Outlier or model of austerity in Europe? The case of Irish social protection reform', *Social Policy and Administration*, 48(4): 413–29.

Dukelow, F. and Kennett, P. (2018) 'Discipline, debt and coercive commodification: Post-crisis neoliberalism and the welfare state in Ireland, the UK and the USA', *Critical Social Policy*, 38(3): 482–504.

Ehrler, F. (2012) 'New public governance and activation', *International Journal of Sociology and Social*, 32(5/6): 327–39.

European Commission (2011) *The Economic Adjustment Programme for Ireland*. Occasional Papers 76, Brussels: European Commission.

Evans, T. (2016) 'Professionals and discretion in street-level bureaucracy', in P. Hupe, M. Hill, and A. Buffat (eds) *Understanding Street-Level Bureaucracy*. Bristol: Policy Press, pp 279–94.

Evetts, J. (2011) 'A new professionalism? Challenges and opportunities', *Current Sociology*, 59(4): 406–22.

Evetts, J. (2013) 'Professionalism: value and ideology', *Current Sociology*, 61(5–6): 778–96.

Finn, D. (2010) 'Outsourcing employment programmes: Contract design and differential prices', *European Journal of Social Security*, 12(4): 289–302.

Finn, P. (2021) 'Navigating indifference: Irish jobseekers' experiences of welfare conditionality', *Administration*, 69(2): 67–86.

Fuertes, V. and Lindsay, C. (2016) 'Personalisation and street-level practice in activation: the case of the UK's Work Programme', *Public Administration*, 94(2): 526–41.

Fuertes, V., McQuaid, R., and Robertson, P.J. (2021) 'Career-first: An approach to sustainable labour market integration', *International Journal for Educational and Vocational Guidance*, 21(2): 429–46.

Gaffney, S. and Millar, M. (2020) 'Rational skivers or desperate strivers? The problematisation of fraud in the Irish social protection system', *Critical Social Policy*, 40(1): 69–88.

Gale, N.K., Heath, G., Cameron, E., Rashid, S., and Redwood, S. (2013) 'Using the framework method for the analysis of qualitative data in multi-disciplinary health research', *BMC Medical Research Methodology*, 3(1): 117.

Gerards, R. and Welters, R. (2022) 'Does eliminating benefit eligibility requirements improve unemployed job search and labour market outcomes?', *Applied Economics Letters*, 29(10): 955–58.

Gingrich, J. (2011) *Making Markets in the Welfare State: The Politics of Varying Market Reforms*. Cambridge: Cambridge University Press.

Government of Ireland (2011) *Government for National Recovery 2011–16*. Dublin: Government of Ireland.

Government of Ireland (2012) *Pathways to Work 2012–16*. Dublin: Government of Ireland.

Government of Ireland (2021) *Pathways to Work 2021–25*. Dublin: Government of Ireland.

Greer, I. (2016) 'Welfare reform, precarity and the re-commodification of labour', *Work, Employment and Society*, 31(1): 162–73.

Greer, I., Breidahl, K., Knuth, M., and Larsen, F. (2017) *The Marketisation of Employment Services: The Dilemmas of Europe's Work-First Welfare States*. Oxford: Oxford University Press.

Greer, I., Schulte, L., and Symon, G. (2018) 'Creaming and parking in marketised employment services: An Anglo-German comparison', *Human Relations*, 71(11): 1427–53.

Grover, C. (2009) 'Privatizing employment services in Britain', *Critical Social Policy*, 29(3): 487–509.

Grover, C. (2019). 'Violent proletarianisation: Social murder, the reserve army of labour and social security "austerity" in Britain', *Critical Social Policy*, 39(3): 335–55.

Grubb, D., Singh, S., and Tergeist, P. (2009) *Activation Policies in Ireland*. Paris: OECD.

Hasenfeld, Y. (2010) 'Organisational responses to social policy: The case of welfare reform', *Administration in Social Work*, 34(2): 148–67.

Hemerijck, A. (2015) 'The quiet paradigm revolution of social investment', *Social Politics*, 22(2): 242–56.

Hick, R. (2018) 'Enter the Troika: The politics of social security during Ireland's bailout', *Journal of Social Policy*, 47(1): 1–20.

Hick, R. and Murphy, M.P. (2021) 'Common shock, different paths? Comparing social policy responses to COVID-19 in the UK and Ireland', *Social Policy and Administration*, 55(2): 312–15.

Holden, C. (2003) 'Decommodification and the workfare state', *Political Studies Review*, 1(3): 303–16.

House of Commons Work and Pensions Committee (House of Commons) (2015) *Welfare-to-Work: Second Report of Session 2015–16*. London: House of Commons.

Høybye-Mortensen, M. (2015) 'Decision-making tools and their influence on caseworkers' room for discretion', *The British Journal of Social*, 45(2): 600–15.

Indecon (2018) *Indecon Review of Local Employment Services*. Dublin: Indecon Economic Consulting.

Irish National Organisation of the Unemployed (INOU) (2019) *Mapping the journey for unemployed people: report on phase three of the employment services research project*. Dublin: INOU.

Jantz, B. and Klenk, T. (2015) 'Marketisation and managerialisation of active labour market policies in a comparative perspective', in T. Klenk and E. Pavolini (eds) *Restructuring Welfare Governance*. Cheltenham: Elgar, pp 97–117.

Jantz, B., Klenk, T., Larsen, F., and Wiggan, J. (2018) 'Marketisation and varieties of accountability relationships in employment service: comparing Denmark, Germany and Great Britain', *Administration and Society*, 50(3): 321–45.

Jerolmack, C. and Khan, S. (2014) 'Talk is cheap: Ethnography and the attitudinal fallacy', *Sociological Methods and Research*, 43(2): 178–209.

Joint Committee on Social Protection Community and Rural Development and the Islands (Oireachtas Committee) (2021) *Examination of Employment Services: November 2021*. Dublin: Houses of the Oireachtas.

Kallio, J., Blomberg, H., and Kroll, C. (2013) 'Social workers' attitudes towards the unemployed in Nordic countries', *International Journal of Social Welfare*, 22(1): 219–29.

Kaufman, J. (2020) 'Intensity, moderation, and the pressures of expectation: Calculation and coercion in the street-level practice of welfare conditionality', *Social Policy and Administration*, 54(2): 205–18.

Kelly, E., McGuinness, S., Redmond, P. Savage, M., and Walsh, J.R. (2019) *An Initial Evaluation of the Effectiveness of the Intreo Reforms*. Dublin: ESRI.

Kluve, J. (2010) 'The effectiveness of European active labour market programs', *Labour Economics*, 17(6): 904–18.

Knotz, CM. (2018) 'A rising workfare state? Unemployment benefit conditionality in 21 OECD countries, 1980–2012', *Journal of International and Comparative Social Policy*, 34(1): 91–108.

Köppe, S. and MacCarthaigh, M. (2019) 'Public service integration in hard times: Merging unemployment benefit and labour market activation measures', *Administration*, 67(2): 137–60.

Langenbucherm, K. and Vodopivec, M. (2022) *Paying for Results: Contracting Out Employment Services through Outcome-Based Payment Schemes in OECD Countries*. Paris: OECD.

Larsen, F. (2013) 'Active labour-market reform in Denmark', in E.Z. Brodkin and G. Marston (eds) *Work and the Welfare State: Street-Level Organisations and Workfare Politics*. Copenhagen: Djof Publishing, pp 103–24.

Larsen, F. and Wright, S. (2014) 'Interpreting the marketisation of employment services in Great Britain and Denmark', *Journal of European Social Policy*, 24(5): 455–69.

Lasswell, H (1936) *Politics: Who Gets What, When, How*. New York: McGraw-Hill.

Lavelle, O. and Callaghan, N. (2018) *Public Employment Services-Mapping Activation*. Dublin: DPER.

Le Grand, J. (1997) 'Knights, knaves, or pawns? Human behaviour and social policy', *Journal of Social Policy*, 26(2): 149–69.

Le Grand, J. (2010) 'Knights and knaves return: Public service motivation and the delivery of public services', *International Public Management Journal*, 13(1): 56–71.

Le Grand, J. (2011) 'Quasi-market versus state provision of public services: Some ethical considerations', *Public Reason*, 3(2): 80–89.

Le Grand, J. and Bartlett, W. (1993) *Quasi-Markets and Social Policy*. London: Macmillan, pp 1–12.

Lenihan, B. (2009) Financial statement of the Minister for Finance. Available at: https://magill.ie/politics/brian-lenihans-budget-spe ech [accessed 7 March 2022].

Lewis, J.M. (2015) 'The politics and consequences of performance measurement', *Policy and Society*, 34(1): 1–12.

Lewis, J.M., Considine, M., O'Sullivan, S., Nguyen, P., and McGann, M. (2016) *From Entitlement to Experiment: The New Governance of Welfare-to-Work, Australian Report*. Melbourne: Policy Lab.

Lewis, J.M., Considine, M., O'Sullivan, S., Nguyen, P., and McGann, M. (2017) *From Entitlement to Experiment: The New Governance of Welfare-to-Work, UK Report*. Melbourne: Policy Lab.

Lindsay, C., McQuaid, R.W., and Dutton, M. (2007) 'New approaches to employability in the UK: Combining "human capital development" and "work-first" strategies?', *Journal of Social Policy*, 36(4): 539–60.

Lipsky, M. (2010) *Street-Level Bureaucracy: Dilemmas of the Individual in Public Services* (40th Anniversary Edition). New York: Russell Sage.

Lødemel, I. and Gubrium, E. (2014) 'Trajectories of change: activation reforms from inception to times of austerity', in I. Lødemel and A. Moreira (eds) *Activation or Workfare? Governance and the Neo-Liberal Convergence*. Oxford: Oxford University Press, pp 327–48.

Lødemel, I. and Moreira, A. (2014) *Activation or Workfare? Governance and the Neo-Liberal Convergence*. Oxford: Oxford University Press.

Loopstra, R., Reeves, A., McKee, M., and Stukler, D. (2015) Do punitive approaches to unemployment benefit recipients increase welfare exit and employment? A cross-sectional analysis of UK sanction reforms. Oxford: Department of Sociology, Oxford University.

Lowe, S. (2015) 'JobPath: The proposed introduction of an employment programme in the Republic of Ireland', *The Public Sphere*, 3(2): 113–30.

Marston, G. (2006) 'Employment services in an age of e-government', *Information, Communication and Society*, 9(1): 83–101.

Marston, G. and McDonald, C. (2008) 'Feeling motivated yet? Long-term unemployed people's perspectives on the implementation of workfare in Australia', *Australian Journal of Social Issues*, 43(2): 255–69.

Martin, J.P. (2015) 'Activation and active labour market policies in OECD countries: Stylised facts and evidence on their effectiveness', *IZA Journal of Labour Policy*, 4(4).

Maynard-Moody, S. and Musheno, M. (2000) 'State agent or citizen agent: Two narratives of discretion', *Journal of Public Administration Research and Theory*, 10(2), 329–58.

McDonald, C. and Marston, G. (2005) 'Workfare as welfare: Governing unemployment in the advanced liberal state', *Critical Social Policy*, 25(3): 374–401.

McDonald, C. and Marston, G. (2008) 'Motivating the unemployed? Attitudes at the front line', *Australian Social Work*, 61(4): 315–26.

McGann, M. (2021) '"Double activation": workfare meets marketisation', *Administration*, 69(2): 19–42.

McGann, M. (2022a) 'Meeting the numbers: Performance politics and welfare-to-work at the street-level', *Irish Journal of Sociology*, 30(1): 69–89. DOI: 10.1177/07916035211068430.

McGann, M. (2022b) 'Remodelling street-level workers with quasi-markets: Comparing Ireland's mixed economy of welfare-to-work', *Administration and Society*, 54(5): 939–70. DOI: 10.1177/00953997211050924.

McGann, M., Nguyen, P., and Considine, M. (2020) 'Welfare conditionality and blaming the unemployed'. *Administration and Society*, 52(3): 466–94.

McGann, M., O'Sullivan, S., and Considine, M. (2022) 'Good clients and hard-cases: The role of typologies at the welfare frontline', *Social Services Review*, 96(3): 435–64.

McGuinness, S., O'Connell, P.J., and Kelly, E. (2019) 'Carrots, no stick, no driver: The employment impact of job-search assistance in a regime with minimal monitoring and sanctions', *Journal of Labour Research*, 40(2): 151–80.

Mead, L. (1986) *Beyond Entitlement: The Social Obligations of Citizenship*. New York: The Free Press.

Mead, L. (2014) 'The new politics of the new poverty', in C. Pierson, F.G. Castles, and I.K. Naumann (eds) *The Welfare State Reader* (3rd edition). Cambridge: Polity Press, pp 89–99.

Meagher, G. and Goodwin, S. (2015) *Markets, Rights and Power in Australian Social Policy*. Sydney: Sydney University Press.

Mik-Meyer, N. (2018) 'Organisational professionalism: Social workers negotiating tools of NPM', *Professions and Professionalism*, 8(2): e2381.

Morris, L. (2020) 'Activating the welfare subject: The problem of agency', *Sociology*, 54(2): 275–91.

Moynihan, D.P. and Soss, J. (2014) 'Policy feedback and the politics of administration', *Public Administration Review*, 74(3): 320–32.

Murphy, J., Murray, S., Chalmers, J., Martin, S., and Marston, G. (2011) *Half a Citizen: Life on Welfare in Australia*. Sydney: Allen and Unwin.

Murphy, M.P. (2012) 'The politics of Irish labour activation: 1980 to 2010', *Administration*, 60(2): 27–49.

Murphy, M.P. (2016) 'Low-road or high-road? The post-crisis trajectory of Irish activation', *Critical Social Policy*, 36(3): 432–52.

Murphy, M.P. (2018) 'Ode to an invisible woman: The story of qualified adults and partners in Ireland', *Irish Journal of Sociology*, 26(1): 25–45.

Murphy, M.P. and Hearne, R. (2019) 'Implementing marketisation: comparing Irish activation and social housing'. *Irish Political Studies*, 34(3): 444–63.

Murphy, M.P. and McGann, M. (2022) 'A period of contention? The politics of post-crisis activation reform and the creeping marketisation of public employment services', *Irish Political Studies*. DOI: 10.1080/07907184.2022.2044313.

Murray, C. (1984) *Losing Ground*. New York: Basic Books.

National Economic and Social Council (NESC) (2011) *Supports and Services for Unemployed Jobseekers*. Dublin: NESC.

Newman, J. (2007) 'The "double dynamics" of activation: Institutions, citizens and the remaking of welfare governance', *International Journal of Sociology and Social Policy*, 27(9/10): 364–75.

Noordegraaf, M. (2007) 'From "pure" to "hybrid" professionalism: Present-day professionalism in ambiguous public domains', *Administration and Society*, 39(6): 761–85.

Noordegraaf, M. (2015) 'Hybrid professionalism and beyond: (New) forms of public professionalism in changing organisational and societal contexts', *Journal of Professions and Organisation*, 2(2): 187–206.

Nothdurfter, U. (2016) 'The street-level delivery of activation policies: Constraints and possibilities for a practice of citizenship', *European Journal of Social Work*, 19(3–4): 420–40.

Organisation for Economic Co-operation and Development (OECD) (2022) Public spending on labour markets. Available at: https://data.oecd.org/socialexp/public-spending-on-labour-markets.htm [accessed 3 March 2022].

Osborne, D. (1993) 'Reinventing government', *Public Productivity and Management Review*, 16(4): 349-56.

O'Sullivan, S., McGann, M., and Considine, M. (2019) 'The category game and its impact on street-level bureaucrats and jobseekers: An Australian case study', *Social Policy and Society*, 18(4): 631–65.

O'Sullivan, S., McGann, M., and Considine, M. (2021) *Buying and Selling the Poor: Inside Australia's Privatised Welfare-to-Work Market*. Sydney: Sydney University Press.

Patrick, R. (2012) 'Work as the primary "duty" of the responsible citizen: a critique of this work-centric approach', *People, Place & Policy Online*, 6(1): 5–15.

Pattaro, S., Bailey, N., Williams, E., Gibson, M., Wells, V., Tranmer, M., and Dibben, C. (2022) 'The impacts of benefit sanctions: A scoping review of the quantitative research evidence', *Journal of Social Policy*. DOI: 0.1017/S0047279421001069.

Payne, D. and McCashin, A. (2005) *Welfare State Legitimacy: The Republic of Ireland in Comparative Perspective*. Dublin: Geary Institute Discussion Paper Series.

Peck, J. (2001) *Workfare States*. New York: Guildford.

Peck, J. and Theodore, N. (2000) '"Work-first": workfare and the regulation of contingent labour markets', *Cambridge Journal of Economics*, 24(1): 119–38.

Ponnert, L. and Svensson, K. (2015) 'Standardisation-the end of professional discretion?', *European Journal of Social Work*, 19(3–4): 586–99.

Power, M.J., Devereux, E., and Ryan, M. (2022) 'Framing and shaming: The 2017 welfare cheats, cheat us all campaign', *Social Policy and Society*, 21(4): 646–56.

Raffass, T. (2016) 'Work enforcement in liberal democracies', *Journal of Social Policy*, 45(3): 417–34.

Raffass, T. (2017) 'Demanding activation', *Journal of Social Policy*, 46(2): 349–65.

Redman, J. and Fletcher, D.R. (2021). 'Violent bureaucracy: A critical analysis of the British public employment service', *Critical Social Policy*, 42(2): 306–26.

Redmond, P. (2020) *Minimum Wage Policy in Ireland*. Dublin: ESRI.

Regan, A. (2013) *The Impact of the Eurozone Crisis on Irish Social Partnership: A Political Economy Analysis*. Geneva: International Labour Organisation.

Rice, D. (2013) 'Street-level bureaucrats and the welfare state: toward a micro-institutionalist theory of policy implementation', *Administration and Society*, 45(9): 1038–62.

Rice, D. (2017) 'How governance conditions affect the individualisation of active labour market services: An exploratory vignette study', *Public Administration*, 95(2): 468–81.

Roche, Z. and Griffin, R. (2022) 'Activation through marketisation as a process of ignorancing', Social Policy and Administration. DOI: 10.1111/SPOL.12871.

Sadeghi, T. and Fekjær, S. (2018) 'Frontline workers' competency in activation work', *International Journal of Social Welfare*, 28(1): 77–88.

Sainsbury, R. (2017) 'Activation in the UK: the frontline and the "black box" of employment service provision', in R. van Berkel, D. Caswell, P. Kupka, and F. Larsen (eds) *Frontline Delivery of Welfare-to-Work Policies in Europe*. New York: Routledge, pp 53–69.

Schram, S. (2012) 'Welfare professionals and street-level bureaucrats', in M. Gray, J. Midgely, and S. Webb (eds) *The Sage Handbook of Social Work*. Los Angeles: Sage, pp 67–80.

Schram, S. and Silverman, B. (2012) 'The end of social work: Neo-liberalising social policy implementation', *Critical Policy Studies*, 6(2): 128–45.

Seikel, D. and Spannagel, D. (2018) 'Activation and in-work poverty', in H. Lohmann and I. Marx (eds) *Handbook on In-Work Poverty*. Cheltenham: Elgar, pp 245–60.

Select Committee on Social Protection, Community and Rural Development and the Islands (Select Committee) (2021) Proposed Regional Employment Service: discussion, 16 June 2021. Available at: https://www.oireachtas.ie/en/debates/debate/select_committee_on_social_protection_community_and_rural_development_and_the_islands/2021-06-16/5/ [accessed 2 July 2021].

Shutes, I. and Taylor, R. (2014) 'Conditionality and the financing of employment services: Implications for the social divisions of work and welfare', *Social Policy and Administration*, 48(2): 204–20.

Soss, J., Fording, R., and Schram, S. (2011a) *Disciplining the Poor: Neoliberal Paternalism and the Persistent Power of Race*. Chicago: University of Chicago Press.

Soss, J., Fording, R., and Schram, S. (2011b) 'The organisation of discipline: From performance management to perversity and punishment', *Journal of Public Administration Research and Theory*, 21(supplement): i203–32.

Soss, J., Fording, R., and Schram, S. (2013) 'Performance management as a disciplinary regime: Street-level organisations in a neoliberal era of poverty governance', in E.Z. Brodkin and G. Marston (eds) *Work and the Welfare State: Street-Level Organisations and Workfare Politics*. Copenhagen: Djof, pp 125–42.

Stambe, R. and Marston, G. (2022) 'Checking activation at the door: Rethinking the welfare-work nexus in light of Australia's COVID-19 Response', *Social Policy and Society*. DOI: 10.1017/S1474746421000944.

Struyven, L. and Steurs, G. (2005) 'Design and redesign of a quasi-market for the reintegration of jobseekers: Empirical evidence from Australia and the Netherlands', *Journal of European Social Policy*, 15(3): 211–29.

Talbot, C. (2010) *Theories of Performance: Organisational and Service Improvement in the Public Domain*. Oxford: Oxford University Press.

Taylor, R., Rees, J. and Damm, C. (2016) 'UK employment services: Understanding provider strategies in a dynamic strategic action field', *Policy and Politics*, 44(2): 253–67.

Torfing, J., Andersen, L., Greve, C., and Klausen, K. (2020) *Public Governance Paradigms: Competing and Co-Existing*. Cheltenham: Elgar.

Umney, C., Greer, I., Onaran, Ö., and Symon, G. (2018) 'The state and class discipline: European labour market policy after the financial crisis', *Capital and Class*, 42(2): 333–51.

van Berkel, R. (2013) 'Triple activation: Introducing welfare-to-work into Dutch social assistance', in E.Z. Brodkin and G. Marston (eds) *Work and the Welfare State: Street-Level Organisations and Workfare Politics*. Copenhagen: Djof, pp 87–102.

van Berkel, R. (2017) 'State of the art in frontline studies of welfare-to-work: A literature review', in R. van Berkel, D. Caswell, P. Kupka, and F. Larsen (eds) *Frontline Delivery of Welfare-to-Work Policies in Europe*. New York: Routledge, pp 12–35.

van Berkel, R. and Knies, E. (2016) 'Performance Management, caseloads and the frontline provision of social services', *Social Policy and Administration*, 50(1): 59–78.

van Berkel, R. and Knies, E. (2017) 'The frontline delivery of activation: Workers' preferences and their antecedents', *European Journal of Social Work*, 21(4): 602–15.

van Berkel, R. and van der Aa, P. (2005) 'The marketisation of activation services: A modern panacea? Some lessons from the Dutch experience', *Journal of European Social Policy*, 15(4): 329–43.

van Berkel, R. and van der Aa, P. (2012) 'Activation work: Policy programme administration or professional service provision?', *Journal of Social Policy*, 41(3): 493–510.

van Berkel, R., van der Aa, P., and van Gestel, N. (2010) 'Professionals without a profession? Redesigning case management in Dutch local welfare agencies', *European Journal of Social Work*, 13(4): 447–63.

van Berkel, R., Sager, F., and Ehrler, F. (2012) 'The diversity of activation markets in Europe', *International Journal of Sociology and Social Policy*, 32(1): 273–85.

van Berkel, R., de Vries, J., and van der Aa, P. (2021) 'Practising professionalism in activation work: Developing and testing a questionnaire', *International Journal of Social Welfare*, 31(2): 139–53.

Wacquant, L. (2012) 'Three steps to a historical anthropology of actually existing neoliberalism', *Social Anthropology*, 20(1): 66–79.

Whelan, J. (2021) 'Work and thrive or claim and skive: Experiencing the "toxic symbiosis" of worklessness and welfare recipiency in Ireland', *Irish Journal of Sociology*, 29(1): 3–31.

Whelan, J. (2022) *Hidden Voices: Lived Experiences in the Irish Welfare Space*. Bristol: Policy Press.

Whelan, N. (2021) 'Opening the black box of implementing activation in Ireland', *Administration*, 69(2): 87–106.

Whelan, N., Murphy, M.P., and McGann, M. (2021) 'The enabling role of employment guidance in contemporary public employment services: A work-first to life-first typology', *British Journal of Guidance and Counselling*, 49(2): 200–12.

Whitworth, A. and Carter, E. (2014) 'Welfare-to-work reform, power and inequality: From governance to governmentalities', *Journal of Contemporary European Studies*, 22(2): 104–17.

Whitworth, A. and Carter, E. (2020) 'Programme form and service-user well-being: Linking theory and evidence', *Social Policy and Administration*, 54(5): 844–58.

Wiggan, J. (2015a) 'Varieties of marketisation in the UK: Examining divergence in activation markets between Great Britain and Northern Ireland 2008–2014', *Policy Studies*, 36(2): 115–32.

Wiggan, J. (2015b) 'What variety of employment service quasi-market? Ireland's JobPath as a private power market', *Social Policy Review*, 27: 151–65.

Wright, S. (2012) 'Welfare-to-work, agency and personal responsibility', *Journal of Social Policy*, 42(2): 309–28.

Wright, S., Fletcher, D., and Stewart, A. (2020) 'Punitive benefit sanctions, welfare conditionality, and the social abuse of unemployed people in Britain: Transforming claimants into offenders?', *Social Policy and Administration*, 54(2): 278–94.

Zacka, B. (2017) *When the State Meets the Street: Public Service and Moral Agency*. Cambridge, MA: Belknap Press.

Index

References to figures and tables appear in *italic*.